MW00534195

a personalized record of your
messages from the universe

The
Oracle
Card
JOURNAL

maria sofia marmanides

ADAMS MEDIA
New York London Toronto Sydney New Delhi

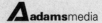

Adams Media
An Imprint of Simon & Schuster, Inc.
100 Technology Center Drive
Stoughton, Massachusetts 02072

First Adams Media hardcover edition November 2022

ADAMS MEDIA and colophon are trademarks of Simon & Schuster.

For information about special discounts for bulk purchases, please contact Simon & Schuster Special Sales at 1-866-506-1949 or business@simonandschuster.com.

The Simon & Schuster Speakers Bureau can bring authors to your live event. For more information or to book an event contact the Simon & Schuster Speakers Bureau at 1-866-248-3049 or visit our website at www.simonspeakers.com.

Interior design and illustrations by Priscilla Yuen

Manufactured in the United States of America

1 2022

ISBN 978-1-5072-1984-3

To the bird in Oxford.

Acknowledgments

I must first offer my sincerest and most heartfelt thanks to the team at Adams Media, especially Rebecca Tarr Thomas and Sarah Doughty for working with me and bringing this book to life. You both have made my literary and lifelong dreams come true—twice.

I'd like to thank my friends for their enthusiastic support, especially: LPR, NM, MY, HMS, AEF, TBB, CKM, DD, AJ, SDB, ST, and SNC. ER: Thank you from the bottom of my heart and soul.

Mom, Dad, Val, John, and Fifi: Thank you for lifetimes together.

Joanne: Thank you for listening.

Finally, I'd like to thank the bird in Oxford, CT, who paid special attention to me that unassuming but ultimately auspicious day in July 2021—and to DW for confirming it was, indeed, good luck.

Contents

Introduction

Do you wonder what your soul purpose is? Whether you will ever have your dream job? Or simply what's going to happen next in your life?

The Oracle Card Journal is your guide to divining the answers you seek. Everyone has questions. And by connecting with your intuition and spirit guides, or divine beings, you *can* satisfy those burning inquiries. In fact, people have been doing this for centuries; the practice of going to see an oracle (a person who acts as a messenger for spirits, deities, or other mystical entities) to receive an answer to a question was quite common in ancient times. And it continues today, with oracle cards. All it takes to become your own oracle is an open mind, an oracle deck, and this journal (and a pen or pencil too)!

In Part 1, you will get to know more about oracle cards, from what they are and how they work, to what sets them apart from tarot cards. You'll also discover how journaling can help you grow as an intuitive reader of the deck. You'll learn how to complete an oracle card reading in three easy steps:

1 Clear your mind to focus on the cards.
2 Meditate on your question as you shuffle the cards.
3 Draw a card and reflect on the answer it gives.

In Part 2, you'll discover how to phrase your question in a clear way and how to use this journal to intuit the answer, as well as key tips for making the most of your journaling experience. Then, you'll use the open journal entries provided in this part to record your own oracle card readings.

With this book and oracle cards, you'll uncover the answers to all your burning questions and take control over your life's story. Your journey to connecting to your higher intuitive power starts now!

part one

Oracle Card Basics

In ancient times, people took great pains to gain access to oracles who they believed were able to predict the future. They saw oracles as prophets, as voices of the gods, and they regarded these powerful beings as channels to higher wisdom from the cosmos. Oracles would be consulted for any number of topics both personal and political, like prospects for marriage, war, business, health, and more—and their likely outcomes. So how does this ancient practice translate to our modern world? Here's the secret: You already have the same access to these divinatory prophecies that your ancestors did—all without having to leave your house or use a time machine—thanks to the power of oracle cards!

With the insight and instruction provided in this part, you will find out for yourself how to become your own oracle and answer any question you have with the simple practice of drawing and reflecting on a card.

chapter one

An Introduction to Oracle Cards

Oracle cards are any deck of cards that can be used as a divination tool—meaning, to access information about a past, current, or future situation—and as a means of self-reflection and introspection. They use symbolic imagery and keywords that are inherently designed to answer and align with the question being asked of them. Through a magical, alchemical process, when you ask your oracle cards a question, you can trust that the answer you most need to hear in that moment will present itself to you. By using oracle cards, you gain insight, wisdom, comfort, and clarity. You are guided to use your free will to take the next best course of action.

So how exactly do oracle cards work? And are the messages you receive your subconscious speaking to you? Or a higher power? Or maybe a little bit of both? In this chapter, you'll find out just how this magical practice works—and how it can change your life in all the best ways.

∙ ✦ How Do Oracle Cards Work? ✦ ∙∙

The word "oracle" comes from the Latin verb "to speak." And that's exactly what you're doing every time you consult the cards and ask them for guidance. You're "speaking" with the oracle through the cards in front of you. Engaging in this conversation is both human and divine: Oracle cards give you access to information from a higher power, but to interpret that information, you are invited to tap in to your own intuitive and subconscious powers. Like talking to, confiding in, or consulting a trusted friend, advisor, counselor, or therapist, oracle cards offer guidance. They're not telling you what to do or handing you a doomsday prophecy that is guaranteed to happen regardless of what you do: They're conversing with you from a loving place and hoping you'll do what is best for *you*.

The practice of oracle card reading is often referred to as *cartomancy*, a fancy way of saying "predicting the future" or "divining meaning" using playing cards, tarot cards, or, in this case, oracle cards. Like all cartomancy-based tools, oracle cards can help you unlock answers to questions that have previously seemed unknowable or inaccessible—all by asking simple and direct questions to the deck and then interpreting the answer you receive. It can be literal, but often the magic happens in synthesizing the symbolism of the card's meaning and your instinctive, intuitive reactions.

✦ Why Should You Use Oracle Cards? ✦

As a human being on this earth, you have an innate right to ask questions of the Universe. And it's not a one-sided conversation! How the Universe responds to your individual curiosity about your life, its meaning, and your place in the cosmos—and how it opens your intuition and points to what you understand deep inside—is all part of your soul's journey in this lifetime.

Therefore, think of your curiosity as a gift. Ask questions. Ask as many questions as you'd like. The more curious—and less judgmental—you remain, the more fulfilling you can make ordinary events in your life feel. Oracle cards let you know that you can navigate any situation—even the most challenging ones—with more grace and understanding, and with a deep knowing that there is purpose to your life.

And consider how unsatisfying it would be if someone told you exactly how everything was going to happen, regardless of your own actions. Like spoiling a favorite show or movie, you then wouldn't necessarily want to watch the ending, or at least you wouldn't enjoy it as much, would you? Imagine if the oracle just blurted out an exact timeline of events in your life. How utterly boring would that be? How robbed of catharsis would you feel—not to mention how powerless to shape your own future?

It's by using oracle cards that you see they aren't about "predicting" the future with literal accuracy. They *can*, should you choose to continue down a certain path they give insights into...but still, even in that case, the magic is in the process—and in your participation.

You're like a detective who has been given clues—sacred clues so you know you're following the right scent. Using oracle cards is a very personal process of asking the right questions to align you with your soul path. Your destiny. It's understanding your part in the divine wisdom of the Universe—and that, as mentioned previously, you have a right to know things. You have a right to access a higher power, one you can tap in to whenever you desire, by learning how to find the inner core of truth already inside you. That way, when you confront the situation suggested in an oracle card reading, and see it playing out in real time, you truly understand how you are part of something greater than yourself.

Becoming your own oracle means knowing that the Universe is watching out for you and has a plan.

··✦ How Many Cards Do You Pull? ✦··

There are many different card spreads you can draw for an oracle card reading; however, this journal is designed to help you keep it simple by using the one card method. You can glean a ton of insight from using just one card to answer your question. It's as simple as grounding yourself before your reading, asking a question and pulling a card to answer it, and then meditating on the answer and journaling about it. It is when you pull one card and reflect on its specific message that the magic of oracle cards comes to life. No elaborate card spreads or complex questions. One question, one answer, and done. It really can be that easy. (You will explore each step of the process—grounding, meditating, and journaling—in more detail in Chapter 2.)

$\cdot \bullet \mathbf{+}$ How Are Oracle Cards Different $\mathbf{+} \bullet \cdot$ from Tarot Cards?

Like tarot cards, oracle cards can be consulted any time you have a question, but unlike tarot cards, there are far fewer rules or traditional definitions to understand in oracle card readings.

While tarot is based on a seventy-eight-card system with subsets of cards (the Major and Minor Arcana), an oracle deck is made up of an indeterminate number of nonspecific cards, depending on the creator's intention and discretion. Each oracle card is inscribed with a main keyword. The oracle card usually includes numbers and imagery, like a tarot card, but some oracle cards contain text only.

Additionally, tarot cards are often used to dig into the background of a question and can shed light on the underlying psychological or emotional energy behind the person asking the question or the situation they are asking about. Oracle cards are often much simpler and more straightforward, depending on the deck you choose. For example, whereas tarot requires more background knowledge of how to interpret pulling the Two of Swords in the context of a love reading, an oracle card is usually more direct, including keywords like "Let go" or "Acceptance." In this way, oracle cards can be used for questions with more clear-cut answers. (More on the kinds of questions to ask your oracle cards in Chapter 2.)

∙∙✦ Why Is Journaling So Important ✦∙∙ for Oracle Card Readings?

One of the most overlooked aspects of using oracle cards is the journaling process. While it may seem like an optional add-on, it is actually an essential piece to building your relationship with the oracle and with your own divinatory and intuitive capabilities. By writing something down, you give it life. It becomes more real. It also communicates to the oracle that you are taking its advice to heart. Journaling is like making a birth certificate of your question—and then seeing how it takes on its own life.

It is also part of a mindful meditation process. As you free-associate your responses to your initial oracle card reading, you will get positive reinforcement on how intuitive you already are, while also seeing over time how much you have continued to flex and expand that psychic muscle. You'll learn more about how to use this oracle journal in Part 2.

chapter two

Using Your Oracle Cards

You've discovered the background and possibilities of oracle cards, and it's time to start reading...almost. First, there are some things you will want to know and likely have questions about—like where exactly do you start in becoming your own oracle? And what kind of deck do you choose?

In this chapter, you will learn the basics for choosing an oracle card deck, as well as the steps for how to use that deck for your personal readings. You'll also find key considerations to keep in mind during every oracle card reading, and how to prepare beforehand to ensure a more effective reading. Throughout this journey, remember that oracle cards are about connecting with your higher wisdom. The guidance in this chapter is designed to keep you from overthinking it.

··✦ Choose Your Oracle Deck ✦··

Before you start doing card readings, you'll need to choose a deck! Visit a local bookstore or metaphysical shop, and/or research online to find an oracle deck you want to work with. As you grow your relationship with your deck, you'll build your interpretative skills and capabilities.

Think of this as your first intuition-building exercise—that just so happens to be super fun to do. The act of choosing your oracle deck is personal. Decks that resonate for some people may not necessarily work for you. You want to look for a deck with a theme that speaks to you first, and then select artwork, imagery, or keywords that you feel a connection to within that chosen theme.

Examples of common oracle decks include:

◆ **Archetypes/Symbols:** Imagery-based decks that are used to guide you into awakening your ability to make symbolic interpretations. With these decks, you are often called to integrate your own experiences with certain symbols and elements—like water, earth, fire, and air, or more specific ones like volcanoes, keys, and lightning—with the creator's vision.

◆ **Occult/Spiritual/Cultural:** Decks designed for those who have a background in, or are practitioners of, a specific religious, spiritual, occult, or regional custom or doctrine. These decks can help you access any of your ancestors or family lineage, or deepen your connection to your practice.

◆ **Goddesses/Angels/Witches/Faeries:** These decks will often feature a figure that is from a spiritual, metaphysical, or fantasy realm. By invoking these beings, you can tap in to a more subconscious, imaginative part of your psyche to help answer your questions.

◆ **Animals/Nature/Crystals:** Decks that feature beings or elements from physical reality may appeal to those who are desiring to feel more grounded, have a more corporeal experience, and/or may want to ask for an overt sign that will manifest in a tangible way (like a message from a specific animal; seeing a bird or a certain type of tree; or deciding on a type of crystal to use for spiritual healing).

◆ **Affirmations/Self-Care:** Often these decks will be about self-empowerment and use a single keyword, mantra, or motivational phrase or quote. While these decks often have their own aesthetic and may include imagery, the focus of the deck is on the text that appears on the cards.

Keep in mind the number of cards in the deck as well. Consider if you like having a higher quantity or prefer a smaller number to grow more intimate with.

👁 Using the Guidebook in Your Deck

After purchasing your oracle deck, you will likely find a printed guidebook included with your cards. This guidebook will have descriptions with keywords and possibly even interpretations of each card's meaning.

An oracle deck guidebook is intended to be used in two ways. First, it can be a helpful starting point to understanding a specific card's meaning or intention. You may draw a card and feel stumped, kind of like a card-reader writer's block. In this case, it's a perfect time to refer to the guidebook and see if you get a spark of inspiration for your interpretation and journaling practice.

The second way to use the guidebook is to deepen your understanding of the card you draw. Perhaps you feel confident about what a card is saying or have seen how it manifests in practice. Now see if you can add further detail or dimension to your experience with this card by reading how the creator has written about it. Does it change any thoughts you previously held about the card?

Throughout this process, the key is to remain open-minded and see how understanding a card's original intention and entwining it with your own intuitive application is central to becoming your own oracle.

··✦ Prepare for Your Reading ✦··

As discussed in the previous chapter, unlike other cartomancy systems like tarot, there are very few rules involved in oracle card reading. You may find that the practices of grounding and setting an intention can deepen your connection to your cards and the act of reading them (more on these practices later), but you do not have to create elaborate rituals. You only need three simple things to effectively use oracle cards:

1   A heartfelt question (more on this in later sections).

2   A willingness to receive an honest answer.

3   An open-mindedness to see how the answer manifests.

👁 Grounding Yourself for Oracle Divination

Grounding can help you have a clear mind during oracle divination. If you come to your cards with a sense of over-urgency, panic, dread, fear, or anxiety, that could influence how you interpret the message you receive during your reading. Grounding keeps you focused in the here and now—that way, you can be more objective while conducting your reading without allowing your emotions to influence how you interpret the card (or cards) you draw.

Here are easy steps to ground yourself before a reading:

1   **Choose a comfortable location.** While grounding can be literal, as in going outside and placing your bare feet into the grass, that may not be practical depending on your location or the time of day you're conducting your reading. Instead, you can choose a comfy spot, like a favorite chair, your bed, or any peaceful place you feel safe.

2   **Take a few deep breaths.** If closing your eyes helps with this step, you can do that too. Breathe as you normally would, observing how that feels. When you're ready, on your next inhale, breathe in deeply through your nose, allowing the air to draw downward into your abdomen. Pause for a moment, and then exhale forcefully through your mouth. Repeat this a few times, focusing your attention on your breath entering and exiting your body.

3 Do a creative visualization. Picture yourself in a peaceful environment—a place that conjures up the idea of total relaxation. It could be a made-up place from your imagination or a cherished location from memory. What do you see in this environment? Hear? Feel? Smell? After you've set the scene, enjoy a few minutes here, luxuriating in the experience.

Remember that oracle cards are designed to help you feel more empowered by their insight and information, so even if you are coming to them with a question that feels burning or urgent, try to get grounded into your space before you begin.

◉ Setting Your Intention for Oracle Divination

When you feel called to pull an oracle card, either as part of your daily meditation, as an intuition-building practice, or at a time when you need clear insight into an evolving situation, remember that you are bringing your energy to the session. Therefore, it's important to be intentional about it.

What is it that you want to feel or know after the reading is complete? Do you want advice on what to do? Are you looking for insight on what happened—or what might happen? Do you want to feel more connected to your spirit guides? Do you want comfort and assurance? Being able to identify what is bringing you to seek advice from the oracle will help your readings feel sacred, intentional, and purposeful. And being able to understand your motivations will also help you become clear on the specific question that you want insight on—and how to phrase it.

👁 What to Ask Your Oracle Cards

When it comes to what kinds of questions you can ask the cards, the answer is anything. The question you ask could be about your love life. It could be about your career. It could be about your family. It could be about how your day will turn out. Or it could be what might happen on your next vacation, or how you might feel about selling your house, quitting your job, cutting your hair, or changing your lifestyle. You decide the level of "depth" and importance of the question.

Note that, especially if you're new to the practice of oracle cards, you may find that asking questions that are pertinent to your life but with lower stakes may help you build up your intuitive skills and cartomancy-reading powers. You never have to feel shame around asking questions if they matter to you. "Will this person call me back?" or "Does this person like me?" are valid questions if they are relevant to you. As you grow more comfortable with your ability to understand or predict the answers to less complex questions, you may then feel ready to ask "bigger" spiritual or life-defining questions, like: "What is holding me back from experiencing a soul connection?" or "What do I need to focus on to best support my manifestations?" If the question is heartfelt and important to you, the oracle will answer. Remember that just as you should remain open-minded about how an oracle card's answer may manifest, you should also remain nonjudgmental about yourself for asking it. Be kind to yourself in this process.

EXAMPLE QUESTIONS

How you ask questions is almost as important as what you ask; the more specifically you phrase your question, the clearer the response from the cards will be. Asking a nebulous or meandering question can lead to a less than clear response from your oracle cards.

Spend time thinking about the exact nature of your question and what you truly want an answer to. You may find that in the honing, editing, and crafting process of defining your question, you will get clearer on what part of your situation you actually want clarity on.

Here are some examples of how you can phrase a question for the clearest responses from your oracle cards:

- What is something the Universe or my spirit guides want me to know right now?

- What energy can I focus on right now?

- What is something I can do right now to express myself in a more satisfying way?

- How can I move forward in a way that is most aligned with my wants and needs?

- What word can I embody to have more power [in my relationships/at work/with a specific person]?

- What is coming next for me [in love/in my career/with my family]?

- What is blocking me from being able to receive love?

♦ My relationship with [person] is currently challenging. What can I do to change this dynamic?

♦ What would help me feel happier [at work/in my relationships/ with a specific person]?

Once you have your question crafted and honed, next comes the fun part: You're ready to get started using this journal!

SHOULD YOU OR SHOULD YOU NOT?

At some point during your oracle card journey, you will find yourself wanting to ask a "should" question. "Should I quit?" "Should I break up with my partner?" "Should I tell this person how I feel?" "Should I not go on this trip?" "Should I cancel my plans?"

Many card readers will advise against asking a "should" question because you give up your own personal agency and decision-making abilities to the cards. In this line of thought, you are relinquishing responsibility, and no matter what happens as a result, you can assign credit or blame to the card you chose. ("It's not my fault that this happened because I quit my job—the card told me to do it.")

It is important to remember that as a soul with free will, you are responsible for the choices you make and any consequences, positive or negative, that result from any of the actions (or inactions) you take. Simply put, you are responsible for your life. The cards are tools guiding you to act in alignment with yourself. It's your choice whether to listen, and to decide what you will do with a card's insight.

That being said, only you can decide whether to ask a "should" question, and, similarly, only you can decide what to do based on the reading. Think of "should" questions like a coin toss. As that coin flips in the air, you can gain a lot of insight into what side you want it to land on. No matter what response you get, if you are paying attention to your body and your intuition, you'll know how you feel about the decision you are about to make—if it feels aligned with where you are and gives you a sense of excitement, ease, or optimism, or if it feels like something that is causing you anxiety or filling you with dread or regret. Note that this is part of the process, and that, ultimately, you are always in control of how you choose to act.

·• ✦ Perform Your Reading ✦ •·

Once you have prepared for your reading, it is time to begin! While the next steps will outline what to do while asking your question, shuffling the deck, drawing your card, and reflecting on it, keep in mind that there are no rights or wrongs to the process—just gentle instructions to keep in mind to get the most out of each conversation you have with your oracle cards.

1 **Formulate your question.** What is bringing you to consult your oracle deck? What heartfelt question is weighing on your heart or preoccupying your thoughts? Think through the phrasing of your question.

2 **Shuffle the deck.** As you shuffle your cards, meditate on your situation, and think about your intention, in order to infuse your energy into the deck. State your question out loud or in your mind as you shuffle. Ask that the advice you need at this moment be given to you in the card you draw.

3 **Take a deep breath and then draw your oracle card.** You can decide to cut the deck in half and take the card on the top of one pile. You can fan out all the cards and select the one you feel drawn to. Trust that whichever card you choose is the card you need to see in this moment.

4 **Journal your response.** Write down all your immediate reactions to having pulled this card. How do you feel? What do you think it means? How do you think it will manifest? How does it answer your question in ways that you might expect—or may not be immediately clear about? Has your card unlocked any "aha" moments?

5 **Revisit your journal entries.** Going back to your journal entries after some time has passed—or after you have seen how the card's advice has manifested in your life—will show you two important pieces of information. First, it will show you how much you instinctively and intuitively knew already, and second, it will show how the oracle may have also revealed a piece of information you hadn't considered and can see now in retrospect. It's the most fun—and satisfying—part of this process.

⋅• ✦ Flex Your Intuitive Muscle ✦ •⋅

You've explored the basics of oracle cards and how to do a reading and what kinds of questions to ask the cards, and now you're ready to begin your own card readings. As you draw cards and journal, you will be able to see just how psychic you've always been, while also strengthening your natural intuitive muscle even more with each new oracle card reading and reflection. Let's get started, oracle!

part two

Journaling with Oracle Cards

Now that you understand the basics of oracle cards, including the history of divination and how you can use the same prophetic, ancient wisdom and apply its learnings to modern life through oracle cards and journaling, it's time to start filling out your oracle card journal!

In this part, you'll learn best practices for journaling and more on the one card reading, which is the method used in this journal. You'll find examples of questions to ask, and information on exactly what to do once you've finished your reading and journaling practices for a question. This journal was designed to guide you in keeping your oracle readings simple and easy to understand, and your journaling focused and illuminating. Are you ready to become your own oracle? The mystical worlds of the divine and your own subconscious await.

⋅ ∙ ✦ How to Use This Journal ✦ ∙ ⋅

This oracle card journal is for you to use to ask your most pressing or heartfelt questions. Ask whatever it is that is weighing on you, draw an oracle card using the steps outlined in Chapter 2, and then reflect on the answer you receive using the lines provided. Later, when you feel called to do so, you can come back to your journal entry and see how you have changed since you initially asked the oracle your question. Only then does it become a fully lived, multi-dimensional experience.

You are encouraged to use this journal as it suits you. If you would like to use it for daily journaling as you build your relationship with your chosen deck, you can do so. Alternatively, you can use this journal to get answers to specific questions you ask your oracle cards less frequently. You may decide you only want to use oracle cards when you're facing a particularly challenging situation. This can be when you're struggling to make a decision between two options, or you feel anxious about the outcome of a certain event and want spiritually based reassurance or insight into what you can expect.

👁 Filling Out Your Journal

Just like taking notes in class helped you remember and retain information in school, the act of recording your oracle card readings gives you an advantage in becoming your own oracle faster and with more confidence.

Each journal entry is purposefully designed to be free-form. It allows you to set your intention, ask your question, and record your reflection as you wish. Part of journaling means that sometimes you'll have an instant connection, and the answer seems so clear. That's great! And other times, you'll need some time to think creatively about how the card is answering your question. No matter what you see on TV, in movies, or scrolling through social media, you do not have to have an instant answer. Like you learned in Chapter 2, there is no right or wrong way for you to be your own oracle. This process is designed to help you develop your own style and see what works for you.

Before you begin journaling, read through the following tips, and keep these in mind to help you get the most out of oracle card journaling.

- **When to do a reading:** Whenever you have a question you would like a heartfelt answer to, and when you have time to meditate on your question and journal about your response.

- **What to record about your reading:** The date you asked the question, the specific question you asked, the type of deck you used for the reading, the card you received, the answer reflected in that card, and how you feel about that answer.

- **What to do after recording your reading:** Carry on with your life as you normally would, while making intentional space in your subconscious mind for the oracle to reveal to you how the answer will manifest and how the situation will unfold.

ADDITIONAL TIPS

♦ **Be honest with yourself.** It's okay to feel disappointed about the card you draw. In fact, you can gain a lot of insight about your situation and how you feel about it (and what you may want to do about it) when you get an answer that doesn't align with what you thought you wanted. That's an essential part of the process!

♦ **Don't rush to judgment.** Sometimes you may draw a card and feel an instant sense of understanding, like the proverbial eureka moment. ("Aha! The answer has been right in front of me this entire time!") Other times, you may receive an answer and feel a bit stumped by what it means. Whatever your experience, don't rush to a certain conclusion without giving it time and deeper thought. Think of your oracle card like a key that is unlocking the mystery—not the mystery itself. It's your clue about what might happen next in the physical world; a literal or figurative sign to look out for; or a main component of how you subconsciously feel. Be open to how it may manifest. If you need to close your journal and walk away for a bit, do that. You might find that by not focusing on it, your subconscious will push the message to your conscious mind when you're not noticing.

♦ **Consider a different perspective.** Should you feel unsure or like you're questioning your intuition, first know that's part of the process and that every reader, no matter their skill level, feels this at times. That's what the "Additional Questions for Further Reflection" section at the end of each journal entry is for: to allow you to consider the card you drew from a different perspective and help prompt you to see what may be making you feel stuck.

·· ✦ **Becoming Your Own Oracle** ✦ ··

You're ready to start your journey to using these fun, beautiful, and magical cards so that you can be your own oracle. As you read, reflect, and record, you'll learn how personally gratifying it is to be able to answer your own questions through the gentle counsel of your spirit guides coaxing information from your subconscious into your consciousness. You'll see the different, creative, and often clever and unexpected ways the oracle cards answer your questions. You'll feel more connected and aligned between your mind, body, and spirit. Finally, you'll know that there is a design to your life, and that you are cared for and protected, no matter what kinds of situations you're facing. All you have to do is be patient with yourself—and trust the process.

✦ ·· journal entry ·· ✦

date _____ time _____

deck _____

QUESTION ASKED

_____
_____

card pulled _____

REFLECTION

_____
_____
_____
_____
_____
_____
_____
_____
_____
_____
_____

ADDITIONAL QUESTIONS FOR FURTHER REFLECTION

How do you interpret the message you received?

Can you use the oracle card's keyword in a sentence to describe how you feel?

Does the card's message resonate with the question asked? Why or why not? (Note that the answer can change when you refer to this entry later.)

What artwork, if any, on your selected card spoke to you?

✦ journal entry ✦

date _____   time _____

deck _____

QUESTION ASKED

_____
_____

card pulled _____

REFLECTION

_____
_____
_____
_____
_____
_____
_____
_____
_____
_____
_____

ADDITIONAL QUESTIONS FOR FURTHER REFLECTION

How do you interpret the message you received?

*Can you use the oracle card's keyword in a sentence
to describe how you feel?*

*Does the card's message resonate with the question asked?
Why or why not? (Note that the answer can change when
you refer to this entry later.)*

What artwork, if any, on your selected card spoke to you?

journal entry

date _____   time _____

deck _____

QUESTION ASKED

_____

_____

card pulled _____

REFLECTION

_____

_____

_____

_____

_____

_____

_____

_____

_____

_____

ADDITIONAL QUESTIONS FOR FURTHER REFLECTION

How do you interpret the message you received?

*Can you use the oracle card's keyword in a sentence
to describe how you feel?*

*Does the card's message resonate with the question asked?
Why or why not? (Note that the answer can change when
you refer to this entry later.)*

What artwork, if any, on your selected card spoke to you?

✦ journal entry ✦

date _____   time _____

deck _____

QUESTION ASKED

_____
_____

card pulled _____

REFLECTION

_____
_____
_____
_____
_____
_____
_____
_____
_____
_____
_____

ADDITIONAL QUESTIONS FOR FURTHER REFLECTION

How do you interpret the message you received?

*Can you use the oracle card's keyword in a sentence
to describe how you feel?*

*Does the card's message resonate with the question asked?
Why or why not? (Note that the answer can change when
you refer to this entry later.)*

What artwork, if any, on your selected card spoke to you?

✦ ⋅⋅ journal entry ⋅⋅ ✦

date _____ time _____

deck _____

QUESTION ASKED

_____

_____

card pulled _____

REFLECTION

_____

_____

_____

_____

_____

_____

_____

_____

_____

_____

ADDITIONAL QUESTIONS FOR FURTHER REFLECTION

How do you interpret the message you received?

*Can you use the oracle card's keyword in a sentence
to describe how you feel?*

*Does the card's message resonate with the question asked?
Why or why not? (Note that the answer can change when
you refer to this entry later.)*

What artwork, if any, on your selected card spoke to you?

◆·· journal entry ··◆

date _____   time _____

deck _____

_____
_____

card pulled _____

REFLECTION

_____
_____
_____
_____
_____
_____
_____
_____
_____
_____

ADDITIONAL QUESTIONS FOR FURTHER REFLECTION

How do you interpret the message you received?

*Can you use the oracle card's keyword in a sentence
to describe how you feel?*

*Does the card's message resonate with the question asked?
Why or why not? (Note that the answer can change when
you refer to this entry later.)*

What artwork, if any, on your selected card spoke to you?

✦ ✦ journal entry ✦ ✦

date _____ time _____

deck _____

_____

_____

card pulled _____

REFLECTION

_____

_____

_____

_____

_____

_____

_____

_____

_____

_____

_____

_____

ADDITIONAL QUESTIONS FOR FURTHER REFLECTION

How do you interpret the message you received?

*Can you use the oracle card's keyword in a sentence
to describe how you feel?*

*Does the card's message resonate with the question asked?
Why or why not? (Note that the answer can change when
you refer to this entry later.)*

What artwork, if any, on your selected card spoke to you?

✦ ⋅ journal entry ⋅ ✦

date _____   time _____

deck _____

QUESTION ASKED

_____

_____

card pulled _____

REFLECTION

_____

_____

_____

_____

_____

_____

_____

_____

_____

_____

ADDITIONAL QUESTIONS FOR FURTHER REFLECTION

How do you interpret the message you received?

*Can you use the oracle card's keyword in a sentence
to describe how you feel?*

*Does the card's message resonate with the question asked?
Why or why not? (Note that the answer can change when
you refer to this entry later.)*

What artwork, if any, on your selected card spoke to you?

✦ journal entry ✦

date _____ time _____

deck _____

_____

_____

card pulled _____

REFLECTION

_____

_____

_____

_____

_____

_____

_____

_____

_____

_____

_____

ADDITIONAL QUESTIONS FOR FURTHER REFLECTION

How do you interpret the message you received?

*Can you use the oracle card's keyword in a sentence
to describe how you feel?*

*Does the card's message resonate with the question asked?
Why or why not? (Note that the answer can change when
you refer to this entry later.)*

What artwork, if any, on your selected card spoke to you?

✦ journal entry ✦

date _____ time _____

deck _____

_____

_____

card pulled _____

REFLECTION

_____

_____

_____

_____

_____

_____

_____

_____

_____

_____

_____

ADDITIONAL QUESTIONS FOR FURTHER REFLECTION

How do you interpret the message you received?

*Can you use the oracle card's keyword in a sentence
to describe how you feel?*

*Does the card's message resonate with the question asked?
Why or why not? (Note that the answer can change when
you refer to this entry later.)*

What artwork, if any, on your selected card spoke to you?

✦ journal entry ✦

date _____ time _____

deck _____

_____
_____

card pulled _____

REFLECTION

_____
_____
_____
_____
_____
_____
_____
_____
_____
_____

ADDITIONAL QUESTIONS FOR FURTHER REFLECTION

How do you interpret the message you received?

*Can you use the oracle card's keyword in a sentence
to describe how you feel?*

*Does the card's message resonate with the question asked?
Why or why not? (Note that the answer can change when
you refer to this entry later.)*

What artwork, if any, on your selected card spoke to you?

✦ journal entry ✦

date _____ time _____

deck _____

_____

_____

card pulled _____

REFLECTION

_____

_____

_____

_____

_____

_____

_____

_____

_____

_____

ADDITIONAL QUESTIONS FOR FURTHER REFLECTION

How do you interpret the message you received?

Can you use the oracle card's keyword in a sentence to describe how you feel?

Does the card's message resonate with the question asked? Why or why not? (Note that the answer can change when you refer to this entry later.)

What artwork, if any, on your selected card spoke to you?

✦ · ✦ journal entry ✦ · ✦

date _____   time _____

deck _____

_____

_____

card pulled _____

REFLECTION

_____

_____

_____

_____

_____

_____

_____

_____

_____

_____

_____

ADDITIONAL QUESTIONS FOR FURTHER REFLECTION

How do you interpret the message you received?

*Can you use the oracle card's keyword in a sentence
to describe how you feel?*

*Does the card's message resonate with the question asked?
Why or why not? (Note that the answer can change when
you refer to this entry later.)*

What artwork, if any, on your selected card spoke to you?

✦ journal entry ✦

date _____   time _____

deck _____

_____
_____

card pulled _____

REFLECTION

_____
_____
_____
_____
_____
_____
_____
_____
_____
_____
_____
_____

ADDITIONAL QUESTIONS FOR FURTHER REFLECTION

How do you interpret the message you received?

*Can you use the oracle card's keyword in a sentence
to describe how you feel?*

*Does the card's message resonate with the question asked?
Why or why not? (Note that the answer can change when
you refer to this entry later.)*

What artwork, if any, on your selected card spoke to you?

✦ ⋅⋅ journal entry ⋅⋅ ✦

date _____   time _____

deck _____

QUESTION ASKED

_____
_____

card pulled _____

REFLECTION

_____
_____
_____
_____
_____
_____
_____
_____
_____
_____
_____
_____

ADDITIONAL QUESTIONS FOR FURTHER REFLECTION

How do you interpret the message you received?

*Can you use the oracle card's keyword in a sentence
to describe how you feel?*

*Does the card's message resonate with the question asked?
Why or why not? (Note that the answer can change when
you refer to this entry later.)*

What artwork, if any, on your selected card spoke to you?

✦ ·· journal entry ·· ✦

date _____ time _____

deck _____

QUESTION ASKED

_____
_____

card pulled _____

REFLECTION

_____
_____
_____
_____
_____
_____
_____
_____
_____
_____
_____

ADDITIONAL QUESTIONS FOR FURTHER REFLECTION

How do you interpret the message you received?

*Can you use the oracle card's keyword in a sentence
to describe how you feel?*

*Does the card's message resonate with the question asked?
Why or why not? (Note that the answer can change when
you refer to this entry later.)*

What artwork, if any, on your selected card spoke to you?

✦ ∙ journal entry ∙ ✦

date _____ time _____

deck _____

_____

_____

card pulled _____

REFLECTION

_____

_____

_____

_____

_____

_____

_____

_____

_____

_____

_____

ADDITIONAL QUESTIONS FOR FURTHER REFLECTION

How do you interpret the message you received?

*Can you use the oracle card's keyword in a sentence
to describe how you feel?*

*Does the card's message resonate with the question asked?
Why or why not? (Note that the answer can change when
you refer to this entry later.)*

What artwork, if any, on your selected card spoke to you?

journal entry

date _____ time _____

deck _____

_____

_____

card pulled _____

REFLECTION

_____
_____
_____
_____
_____
_____
_____
_____
_____
_____
_____

ADDITIONAL QUESTIONS FOR FURTHER REFLECTION

How do you interpret the message you received?

Can you use the oracle card's keyword in a sentence to describe how you feel?

Does the card's message resonate with the question asked? Why or why not? (Note that the answer can change when you refer to this entry later.)

What artwork, if any, on your selected card spoke to you?

✦ journal entry ✦

date _____ time _____

deck _____

_____

_____

card pulled _____

REFLECTION

_____

_____

_____

_____

_____

_____

_____

_____

_____

_____

_____

ADDITIONAL QUESTIONS FOR FURTHER REFLECTION

How do you interpret the message you received?

*Can you use the oracle card's keyword in a sentence
to describe how you feel?*

*Does the card's message resonate with the question asked?
Why or why not? (Note that the answer can change when
you refer to this entry later.)*

What artwork, if any, on your selected card spoke to you?

✦ journal entry ✦

date _____   time _____

deck _____

_____

_____

card pulled _____

REFLECTION

_____

_____

_____

_____

_____

_____

_____

_____

_____

_____

_____

ADDITIONAL QUESTIONS FOR FURTHER REFLECTION

How do you interpret the message you received?

*Can you use the oracle card's keyword in a sentence
to describe how you feel?*

*Does the card's message resonate with the question asked?
Why or why not? (Note that the answer can change when
you refer to this entry later.)*

What artwork, if any, on your selected card spoke to you?

✦ ··· journal entry ··· ✦

date _____   time _____

deck _____

QUESTION ASKED

_____

_____

card pulled _____

REFLECTION

_____

_____

_____

_____

_____

_____

_____

_____

_____

_____

_____

ADDITIONAL QUESTIONS FOR FURTHER REFLECTION

How do you interpret the message you received?

*Can you use the oracle card's keyword in a sentence
to describe how you feel?*

*Does the card's message resonate with the question asked?
Why or why not? (Note that the answer can change when
you refer to this entry later.)*

What artwork, if any, on your selected card spoke to you?

✦ ·· journal entry ·· ✦

date _____ time _____

deck _____

QUESTION ASKED

_____
_____

card pulled _____

REFLECTION

_____
_____
_____
_____
_____
_____
_____
_____
_____
_____

ADDITIONAL QUESTIONS FOR FURTHER REFLECTION

How do you interpret the message you received?

*Can you use the oracle card's keyword in a sentence
to describe how you feel?*

*Does the card's message resonate with the question asked?
Why or why not? (Note that the answer can change when
you refer to this entry later.)*

What artwork, if any, on your selected card spoke to you?

✦ ˙ journal entry ˙ ✦

date _____   time _____

deck _____

QUESTION ASKED

_____

_____

card pulled _____

REFLECTION

_____

_____

_____

_____

_____

_____

_____

_____

_____

_____

_____

ADDITIONAL QUESTIONS FOR FURTHER REFLECTION

How do you interpret the message you received?

*Can you use the oracle card's keyword in a sentence
to describe how you feel?*

*Does the card's message resonate with the question asked?
Why or why not? (Note that the answer can change when
you refer to this entry later.)*

What artwork, if any, on your selected card spoke to you?

✦ ·· journal entry ·· ✦

date _____ time _____

deck _____

QUESTION ASKED

_____

_____

card pulled _____

REFLECTION

_____

_____

_____

_____

_____

_____

_____

_____

_____

_____

_____

ADDITIONAL QUESTIONS FOR FURTHER REFLECTION

How do you interpret the message you received?

*Can you use the oracle card's keyword in a sentence
to describe how you feel?*

*Does the card's message resonate with the question asked?
Why or why not? (Note that the answer can change when
you refer to this entry later.)*

What artwork, if any, on your selected card spoke to you?

✦ ·· journal entry ·· ✦

date _____ time _____

deck _____

_____

_____

card pulled _____

REFLECTION

_____

_____

_____

_____

_____

_____

_____

_____

_____

_____

_____

ADDITIONAL QUESTIONS FOR FURTHER REFLECTION

How do you interpret the message you received?

*Can you use the oracle card's keyword in a sentence
to describe how you feel?*

*Does the card's message resonate with the question asked?
Why or why not? (Note that the answer can change when
you refer to this entry later.)*

What artwork, if any, on your selected card spoke to you?

✦ ·· journal entry ·· ✦

date _____   time _____

deck _____

_____

_____

card pulled _____

REFLECTION

_____

_____

_____

_____

_____

_____

_____

_____

_____

_____

ADDITIONAL QUESTIONS FOR FURTHER REFLECTION

How do you interpret the message you received?

*Can you use the oracle card's keyword in a sentence
to describe how you feel?*

*Does the card's message resonate with the question asked?
Why or why not? (Note that the answer can change when
you refer to this entry later.)*

What artwork, if any, on your selected card spoke to you?

✦ ··· journal entry ··· ✦

date _____ time _____

deck _____

_____

_____

card pulled _____

REFLECTION

_____

_____

_____

_____

_____

_____

_____

_____

_____

_____

ADDITIONAL QUESTIONS FOR FURTHER REFLECTION

How do you interpret the message you received?

*Can you use the oracle card's keyword in a sentence
to describe how you feel?*

*Does the card's message resonate with the question asked?
Why or why not? (Note that the answer can change when
you refer to this entry later.)*

What artwork, if any, on your selected card spoke to you?

✦ · journal entry · ✦

date _____   time _____

deck _____

_____

_____

card pulled _____

REFLECTION

_____

_____

_____

_____

_____

_____

_____

_____

_____

_____

_____

ADDITIONAL QUESTIONS FOR FURTHER REFLECTION

How do you interpret the message you received?

*Can you use the oracle card's keyword in a sentence
to describe how you feel?*

*Does the card's message resonate with the question asked?
Why or why not? (Note that the answer can change when
you refer to this entry later.)*

What artwork, if any, on your selected card spoke to you?

✦ · · journal entry · · ✦

date _____   time _____

deck _____

QUESTION ASKED

_____
_____

card pulled _____

REFLECTION

_____
_____
_____
_____
_____
_____
_____
_____
_____
_____
_____

ADDITIONAL QUESTIONS FOR FURTHER REFLECTION

How do you interpret the message you received?

*Can you use the oracle card's keyword in a sentence
to describe how you feel?*

*Does the card's message resonate with the question asked?
Why or why not? (Note that the answer can change when
you refer to this entry later.)*

What artwork, if any, on your selected card spoke to you?

✦ ·· journal entry ·· ✦

date _____ time _____
deck _____

QUESTION ASKED

_____
_____

card pulled _____

REFLECTION

_____
_____
_____
_____
_____
_____
_____
_____
_____
_____
_____

ADDITIONAL QUESTIONS FOR FURTHER REFLECTION

How do you interpret the message you received?

Can you use the oracle card's keyword in a sentence to describe how you feel?

Does the card's message resonate with the question asked? Why or why not? (Note that the answer can change when you refer to this entry later.)

What artwork, if any, on your selected card spoke to you?

✦ ◦ journal entry ◦ ✦

date _____ time _____

deck _____

QUESTION ASKED

_____

_____

card pulled _____

REFLECTION

_____

_____

_____

_____

_____

_____

_____

_____

_____

_____

ADDITIONAL QUESTIONS FOR FURTHER REFLECTION

How do you interpret the message you received?

*Can you use the oracle card's keyword in a sentence
to describe how you feel?*

*Does the card's message resonate with the question asked?
Why or why not? (Note that the answer can change when
you refer to this entry later.)*

What artwork, if any, on your selected card spoke to you?

✦ ·· journal entry ·· ✦

date _____   time _____

deck _____

_____

_____

card pulled _____

REFLECTION

_____
_____
_____
_____
_____
_____
_____
_____
_____
_____

ADDITIONAL QUESTIONS FOR FURTHER REFLECTION

How do you interpret the message you received?

*Can you use the oracle card's keyword in a sentence
to describe how you feel?*

*Does the card's message resonate with the question asked?
Why or why not? (Note that the answer can change when
you refer to this entry later.)*

What artwork, if any, on your selected card spoke to you?

65

✦ ·· journal entry ·· ✦

date _____ time _____

deck _____

_____
_____

card pulled _____

REFLECTION

_____
_____
_____
_____
_____
_____
_____
_____
_____
_____
_____

ADDITIONAL QUESTIONS FOR FURTHER REFLECTION

How do you interpret the message you received?

Can you use the oracle card's keyword in a sentence to describe how you feel?

Does the card's message resonate with the question asked? Why or why not? (Note that the answer can change when you refer to this entry later.)

What artwork, if any, on your selected card spoke to you?

✦ ·· journal entry ·· ✦

date _____   time _____

deck _____

QUESTION ASKED

_____

_____

card pulled _____

REFLECTION

_____

_____

_____

_____

_____

_____

_____

_____

_____

_____

_____

ADDITIONAL QUESTIONS FOR FURTHER REFLECTION

How do you interpret the message you received?

*Can you use the oracle card's keyword in a sentence
to describe how you feel?*

*Does the card's message resonate with the question asked?
Why or why not? (Note that the answer can change when
you refer to this entry later.)*

What artwork, if any, on your selected card spoke to you?

journal entry ✦

date _____ time _____

deck _____

_____

_____

card pulled _____

REFLECTION

_____

_____

_____

_____

_____

_____

_____

_____

_____

_____

_____

ADDITIONAL QUESTIONS FOR FURTHER REFLECTION

How do you interpret the message you received?

*Can you use the oracle card's keyword in a sentence
to describe how you feel?*

*Does the card's message resonate with the question asked?
Why or why not? (Note that the answer can change when
you refer to this entry later.)*

What artwork, if any, on your selected card spoke to you?

journal entry

date _____   time _____

deck _____

_____

_____

card pulled _____

REFLECTION

_____

_____

_____

_____

_____

_____

_____

_____

_____

_____

ADDITIONAL QUESTIONS FOR FURTHER REFLECTION

How do you interpret the message you received?

*Can you use the oracle card's keyword in a sentence
to describe how you feel?*

*Does the card's message resonate with the question asked?
Why or why not? (Note that the answer can change when
you refer to this entry later.)*

What artwork, if any, on your selected card spoke to you?

✦ ⋯ journal entry ⋯ ✦

date _____ time _____

deck _____

_____

_____

card pulled _____

REFLECTION

_____

_____

_____

_____

_____

_____

_____

_____

_____

_____

ADDITIONAL QUESTIONS FOR FURTHER REFLECTION

How do you interpret the message you received?

*Can you use the oracle card's keyword in a sentence
to describe how you feel?*

*Does the card's message resonate with the question asked?
Why or why not? (Note that the answer can change when
you refer to this entry later.)*

What artwork, if any, on your selected card spoke to you?

✦ ·· journal entry ·· ✦

date _____ time _____

deck _____

_____

_____

card pulled _____

REFLECTION

_____

_____

_____

_____

_____

_____

_____

_____

_____

_____

ADDITIONAL QUESTIONS FOR FURTHER REFLECTION

How do you interpret the message you received?

*Can you use the oracle card's keyword in a sentence
to describe how you feel?*

*Does the card's message resonate with the question asked?
Why or why not? (Note that the answer can change when
you refer to this entry later.)*

What artwork, if any, on your selected card spoke to you?

✦ ⋯ journal entry ⋯ ✦

date _____ time _____

deck _____

QUESTION ASKED

_____

_____

card pulled _____

REFLECTION

_____

_____

_____

_____

_____

_____

_____

_____

_____

_____

ADDITIONAL QUESTIONS FOR FURTHER REFLECTION

How do you interpret the message you received?

*Can you use the oracle card's keyword in a sentence
to describe how you feel?*

*Does the card's message resonate with the question asked?
Why or why not? (Note that the answer can change when
you refer to this entry later.)*

What artwork, if any, on your selected card spoke to you?

✦ ⋯ journal entry ⋯ ✦

date _____   time _____

deck _____

_____

_____

card pulled _____

REFLECTION

_____
_____
_____
_____
_____
_____
_____
_____
_____
_____

ADDITIONAL QUESTIONS FOR FURTHER REFLECTION

How do you interpret the message you received?

Can you use the oracle card's keyword in a sentence to describe how you feel?

Does the card's message resonate with the question asked? Why or why not? (Note that the answer can change when you refer to this entry later.)

What artwork, if any, on your selected card spoke to you?

✦ ✦ journal entry ✦ ✦

date _____ time _____

deck _____

_____
_____

card pulled _____

REFLECTION

_____
_____
_____
_____
_____
_____
_____
_____
_____
_____
_____

ADDITIONAL QUESTIONS FOR FURTHER REFLECTION

How do you interpret the message you received?

*Can you use the oracle card's keyword in a sentence
to describe how you feel?*

*Does the card's message resonate with the question asked?
Why or why not? (Note that the answer can change when
you refer to this entry later.)*

What artwork, if any, on your selected card spoke to you?

✦ ⋅ ⋅ journal entry ⋅ ⋅ ✦

date _____   time _____

deck _____

QUESTION ASKED

_____
_____

card pulled _____

REFLECTION

_____
_____
_____
_____
_____
_____
_____
_____
_____
_____
_____

ADDITIONAL QUESTIONS FOR FURTHER REFLECTION

How do you interpret the message you received?

*Can you use the oracle card's keyword in a sentence
to describe how you feel?*

*Does the card's message resonate with the question asked?
Why or why not? (Note that the answer can change when
you refer to this entry later.)*

What artwork, if any, on your selected card spoke to you?

✦ journal entry ✦

date _____   time _____

deck _____

_____

_____

card pulled _____

REFLECTION

_____

_____

_____

_____

_____

_____

_____

_____

_____

_____

_____

_____

ADDITIONAL QUESTIONS FOR FURTHER REFLECTION

How do you interpret the message you received?

*Can you use the oracle card's keyword in a sentence
to describe how you feel?*

*Does the card's message resonate with the question asked?
Why or why not? (Note that the answer can change when
you refer to this entry later.)*

What artwork, if any, on your selected card spoke to you?

✦ ⋆ journal entry ✦ ⋆

date _____ time _____

deck _____

_____
_____

card pulled _____

REFLECTION

_____
_____
_____
_____
_____
_____
_____
_____
_____
_____
_____

ADDITIONAL QUESTIONS FOR FURTHER REFLECTION

How do you interpret the message you received?

*Can you use the oracle card's keyword in a sentence
to describe how you feel?*

*Does the card's message resonate with the question asked?
Why or why not? (Note that the answer can change when
you refer to this entry later.)*

What artwork, if any, on your selected card spoke to you?

✦ • • journal entry • • ✦

date _____ time _____

deck _____

QUESTION ASKED

_____

_____

card pulled _____

REFLECTION

_____

_____

_____

_____

_____

_____

_____

_____

_____

_____

ADDITIONAL QUESTIONS FOR FURTHER REFLECTION

How do you interpret the message you received?

*Can you use the oracle card's keyword in a sentence
to describe how you feel?*

*Does the card's message resonate with the question asked?
Why or why not? (Note that the answer can change when
you refer to this entry later.)*

What artwork, if any, on your selected card spoke to you?

✦ • journal entry • ✦

date _____   time _____

deck _____

QUESTION ASKED

_____

_____

card pulled _____

REFLECTION

_____

_____

_____

_____

_____

_____

_____

_____

_____

_____

_____

ADDITIONAL QUESTIONS FOR FURTHER REFLECTION

How do you interpret the message you received?

*Can you use the oracle card's keyword in a sentence
to describe how you feel?*

*Does the card's message resonate with the question asked?
Why or why not? (Note that the answer can change when
you refer to this entry later.)*

What artwork, if any, on your selected card spoke to you?

✦ •• journal entry •• ✦

date _____ time _____

deck _____

QUESTION ASKED

_____

_____

card pulled _____

REFLECTION

_____

_____

_____

_____

_____

_____

_____

_____

_____

_____

ADDITIONAL QUESTIONS FOR FURTHER REFLECTION

How do you interpret the message you received?

*Can you use the oracle card's keyword in a sentence
to describe how you feel?*

*Does the card's message resonate with the question asked?
Why or why not? (Note that the answer can change when
you refer to this entry later.)*

What artwork, if any, on your selected card spoke to you?

✦ ⋯ journal entry ⋯ ✦

date _____   time _____

deck _____

_____

_____

card pulled _____

REFLECTION

_____

_____

_____

_____

_____

_____

_____

_____

_____

_____

_____

ADDITIONAL QUESTIONS FOR FURTHER REFLECTION

How do you interpret the message you received?

*Can you use the oracle card's keyword in a sentence
to describe how you feel?*

*Does the card's message resonate with the question asked?
Why or why not? (Note that the answer can change when
you refer to this entry later.)*

What artwork, if any, on your selected card spoke to you?

✦ · · journal entry · · ✦

date _____   time _____

deck _____

_____

_____

card pulled _____

REFLECTION

_____
_____
_____
_____
_____
_____
_____
_____
_____
_____
_____
_____

ADDITIONAL QUESTIONS FOR FURTHER REFLECTION

How do you interpret the message you received?

*Can you use the oracle card's keyword in a sentence
to describe how you feel?*

*Does the card's message resonate with the question asked?
Why or why not? (Note that the answer can change when
you refer to this entry later.)*

What artwork, if any, on your selected card spoke to you?

✦ ⋅ journal entry ⋅ ✦

date _____   time _____

deck _____

_____

_____

card pulled _____

_____
_____
_____
_____
_____
_____
_____
_____
_____
_____
_____

ADDITIONAL QUESTIONS FOR FURTHER REFLECTION

How do you interpret the message you received?

Can you use the oracle card's keyword in a sentence to describe how you feel?

Does the card's message resonate with the question asked? Why or why not? (Note that the answer can change when you refer to this entry later.)

What artwork, if any, on your selected card spoke to you?

✦ · journal entry · ✦

date _____   time _____

deck _____

_____
_____

card pulled _____

REFLECTION

_____
_____
_____
_____
_____
_____
_____
_____
_____
_____
_____
_____

ADDITIONAL QUESTIONS FOR FURTHER REFLECTION

How do you interpret the message you received?

*Can you use the oracle card's keyword in a sentence
to describe how you feel?*

*Does the card's message resonate with the question asked?
Why or why not? (Note that the answer can change when
you refer to this entry later.)*

What artwork, if any, on your selected card spoke to you?

✦ ·· journal entry ·· ✦

date _____ time _____

deck _____

QUESTION ASKED

_____
_____

card pulled _____

REFLECTION

_____
_____
_____
_____
_____
_____
_____
_____
_____
_____
_____

ADDITIONAL QUESTIONS FOR FURTHER REFLECTION

How do you interpret the message you received?

*Can you use the oracle card's keyword in a sentence
to describe how you feel?*

*Does the card's message resonate with the question asked?
Why or why not? (Note that the answer can change when
you refer to this entry later.)*

What artwork, if any, on your selected card spoke to you?

◆ ·· journal entry ·· ◆

date _____ time _____

deck _____

QUESTION ASKED

_____
_____

card pulled _____

REFLECTION

_____
_____
_____
_____
_____
_____
_____
_____
_____
_____
_____

ADDITIONAL QUESTIONS FOR FURTHER REFLECTION

How do you interpret the message you received?

*Can you use the oracle card's keyword in a sentence
to describe how you feel?*

*Does the card's message resonate with the question asked?
Why or why not? (Note that the answer can change when
you refer to this entry later.)*

What artwork, if any, on your selected card spoke to you?

journal entry

date _____   time _____

deck _____

_____
_____

card pulled _____

REFLECTION

_____
_____
_____
_____
_____
_____
_____
_____
_____
_____
_____

ADDITIONAL QUESTIONS FOR FURTHER REFLECTION

How do you interpret the message you received?

Can you use the oracle card's keyword in a sentence to describe how you feel?

Does the card's message resonate with the question asked? Why or why not? (Note that the answer can change when you refer to this entry later.)

What artwork, if any, on your selected card spoke to you?

✦ · journal entry · ✦

date _____   time _____

deck _____

_____

_____

card pulled _____

REFLECTION

_____

_____

_____

_____

_____

_____

_____

_____

_____

_____

_____

ADDITIONAL QUESTIONS FOR FURTHER REFLECTION

How do you interpret the message you received?

*Can you use the oracle card's keyword in a sentence
to describe how you feel?*

*Does the card's message resonate with the question asked?
Why or why not? (Note that the answer can change when
you refer to this entry later.)*

What artwork, if any, on your selected card spoke to you?

✦ · · journal entry · · ✦

date _____ time _____

deck _____

QUESTION ASKED

_____

_____

card pulled _____

REFLECTION

_____

_____

_____

_____

_____

_____

_____

_____

_____

_____

ADDITIONAL QUESTIONS FOR FURTHER REFLECTION

How do you interpret the message you received?

*Can you use the oracle card's keyword in a sentence
to describe how you feel?*

*Does the card's message resonate with the question asked?
Why or why not? (Note that the answer can change when
you refer to this entry later.)*

What artwork, if any, on your selected card spoke to you?

✦ • • journal entry • • ✦

date _____ time _____

deck _____

_____

_____

card pulled _____

REFLECTION

_____

_____

_____

_____

_____

_____

_____

_____

_____

_____

_____

ADDITIONAL QUESTIONS FOR FURTHER REFLECTION

How do you interpret the message you received?

*Can you use the oracle card's keyword in a sentence
to describe how you feel?*

*Does the card's message resonate with the question asked?
Why or why not? (Note that the answer can change when
you refer to this entry later.)*

What artwork, if any, on your selected card spoke to you?

✦ • • journal entry • • ✦

date _____   time _____
deck _____

QUESTION ASKED

_____

_____

card pulled _____

REFLECTION

_____
_____
_____
_____
_____
_____
_____
_____
_____
_____

ADDITIONAL QUESTIONS FOR FURTHER REFLECTION

How do you interpret the message you received?

*Can you use the oracle card's keyword in a sentence
to describe how you feel?*

*Does the card's message resonate with the question asked?
Why or why not? (Note that the answer can change when
you refer to this entry later.)*

What artwork, if any, on your selected card spoke to you?

✦ ·✦· journal entry ·✦· ✦

date _____ time _____

deck _____

_____
_____

card pulled _____

REFLECTION

_____
_____
_____
_____
_____
_____
_____
_____
_____
_____
_____
_____

ADDITIONAL QUESTIONS FOR FURTHER REFLECTION

How do you interpret the message you received?

Can you use the oracle card's keyword in a sentence to describe how you feel?

Does the card's message resonate with the question asked? Why or why not? (Note that the answer can change when you refer to this entry later.)

What artwork, if any, on your selected card spoke to you?

✦ ✦ journal entry ✦ ✦

date _____ time _____

deck _____

_____

_____

card pulled _____

REFLECTION

_____

_____

_____

_____

_____

_____

_____

_____

_____

_____

ADDITIONAL QUESTIONS FOR FURTHER REFLECTION

How do you interpret the message you received?

Can you use the oracle card's keyword in a sentence to describe how you feel?

Does the card's message resonate with the question asked? Why or why not? (Note that the answer can change when you refer to this entry later.)

What artwork, if any, on your selected card spoke to you?

✦ ⋅ journal entry ⋅ ✦

date _____ time _____

deck _____

_____

_____

card pulled _____

REFLECTION

_____

_____

_____

_____

_____

_____

_____

_____

_____

_____

_____

ADDITIONAL QUESTIONS FOR FURTHER REFLECTION

How do you interpret the message you received?

*Can you use the oracle card's keyword in a sentence
to describe how you feel?*

*Does the card's message resonate with the question asked?
Why or why not? (Note that the answer can change when
you refer to this entry later.)*

What artwork, if any, on your selected card spoke to you?

✦ ·· journal entry ·· ✦

date _____   time _____

deck _____

_____

_____

card pulled _____

REFLECTION

_____

_____

_____

_____

_____

_____

_____

_____

_____

_____

ADDITIONAL QUESTIONS FOR FURTHER REFLECTION

How do you interpret the message you received?

*Can you use the oracle card's keyword in a sentence
to describe how you feel?*

*Does the card's message resonate with the question asked?
Why or why not? (Note that the answer can change when
you refer to this entry later.)*

What artwork, if any, on your selected card spoke to you?

✦ ∙∙ journal entry ∙∙ ✦

date _____ time _____

deck _____

QUESTION ASKED

_____
_____

card pulled _____

REFLECTION

_____
_____
_____
_____
_____
_____
_____
_____
_____
_____

ADDITIONAL QUESTIONS FOR FURTHER REFLECTION

How do you interpret the message you received?

*Can you use the oracle card's keyword in a sentence
to describe how you feel?*

*Does the card's message resonate with the question asked?
Why or why not? (Note that the answer can change when
you refer to this entry later.)*

What artwork, if any, on your selected card spoke to you?

✦ ·· journal entry ·· ✦

date _____ time _____

deck _____

QUESTION ASKED

_____
_____

card pulled _____

REFLECTION

_____
_____
_____
_____
_____
_____
_____
_____
_____

ADDITIONAL QUESTIONS FOR FURTHER REFLECTION

How do you interpret the message you received?

*Can you use the oracle card's keyword in a sentence
to describe how you feel?*

*Does the card's message resonate with the question asked?
Why or why not? (Note that the answer can change when
you refer to this entry later.)*

What artwork, if any, on your selected card spoke to you?

✦ journal entry ✦

date _____ time _____

deck _____

_____

_____

card pulled _____

REFLECTION

_____

_____

_____

_____

_____

_____

_____

_____

_____

_____

ADDITIONAL QUESTIONS FOR FURTHER REFLECTION

How do you interpret the message you received?

*Can you use the oracle card's keyword in a sentence
to describe how you feel?*

*Does the card's message resonate with the question asked?
Why or why not? (Note that the answer can change when
you refer to this entry later.)*

What artwork, if any, on your selected card spoke to you?

✦ ·· journal entry ··✦

date _____   time _____

deck _____

_____

_____

card pulled _____

REFLECTION

_____

_____

_____

_____

_____

_____

_____

_____

_____

_____

ADDITIONAL QUESTIONS FOR FURTHER REFLECTION

How do you interpret the message you received?

*Can you use the oracle card's keyword in a sentence
to describe how you feel?*

*Does the card's message resonate with the question asked?
Why or why not? (Note that the answer can change when
you refer to this entry later.)*

What artwork, if any, on your selected card spoke to you?

✦ • ✦ journal entry ✦ • ✦

date _____ time _____

deck _____

_____

_____

card pulled _____

REFLECTION

_____

_____

_____

_____

_____

_____

_____

_____

_____

_____

_____

ADDITIONAL QUESTIONS FOR FURTHER REFLECTION

How do you interpret the message you received?

*Can you use the oracle card's keyword in a sentence
to describe how you feel?*

*Does the card's message resonate with the question asked?
Why or why not? (Note that the answer can change when
you refer to this entry later.)*

What artwork, if any, on your selected card spoke to you?

journal entry

date _____   time _____

deck _____

_____

_____

card pulled _____

REFLECTION

_____

_____

_____

_____

_____

_____

_____

_____

_____

_____

_____

ADDITIONAL QUESTIONS FOR FURTHER REFLECTION

How do you interpret the message you received?

*Can you use the oracle card's keyword in a sentence
to describe how you feel?*

*Does the card's message resonate with the question asked?
Why or why not? (Note that the answer can change when
you refer to this entry later.)*

What artwork, if any, on your selected card spoke to you?

✦ · · journal entry · · ✦

date _____   time _____

deck _____

_____

_____

card pulled _____

REFLECTION

_____

_____

_____

_____

_____

_____

_____

_____

_____

_____

_____

ADDITIONAL QUESTIONS FOR FURTHER REFLECTION

How do you interpret the message you received?

*Can you use the oracle card's keyword in a sentence
to describe how you feel?*

*Does the card's message resonate with the question asked?
Why or why not? (Note that the answer can change when
you refer to this entry later.)*

What artwork, if any, on your selected card spoke to you?

✦ ✦ journal entry ✦ ✦

date _____ time _____

deck _____

QUESTION ASKED

_____

_____

card pulled _____

REFLECTION

_____

_____

_____

_____

_____

_____

_____

_____

_____

_____

_____

ADDITIONAL QUESTIONS FOR FURTHER REFLECTION

How do you interpret the message you received?

*Can you use the oracle card's keyword in a sentence
to describe how you feel?*

*Does the card's message resonate with the question asked?
Why or why not? (Note that the answer can change when
you refer to this entry later.)*

What artwork, if any, on your selected card spoke to you?

✦ journal entry ✦

date _____ time _____

deck _____

_____

_____

card pulled _____

REFLECTION

_____

_____

_____

_____

_____

_____

_____

_____

_____

_____

_____

ADDITIONAL QUESTIONS FOR FURTHER REFLECTION

How do you interpret the message you received?

*Can you use the oracle card's keyword in a sentence
to describe how you feel?*

*Does the card's message resonate with the question asked?
Why or why not? (Note that the answer can change when
you refer to this entry later.)*

What artwork, if any, on your selected card spoke to you?

✦ ·· journal entry ·· ✦

date _____ time _____

deck _____

QUESTION ASKED

_____

_____

card pulled _____

REFLECTION

_____

_____

_____

_____

_____

_____

_____

_____

_____

_____

_____

ADDITIONAL QUESTIONS FOR FURTHER REFLECTION

How do you interpret the message you received?

*Can you use the oracle card's keyword in a sentence
to describe how you feel?*

*Does the card's message resonate with the question asked?
Why or why not? (Note that the answer can change when
you refer to this entry later.)*

What artwork, if any, on your selected card spoke to you?

✦ ·· journal entry ·· ✦

date _____ time _____

deck _____

QUESTION ASKED

_____
_____

card pulled _____

REFLECTION

_____
_____
_____
_____
_____
_____
_____
_____
_____
_____
_____

ADDITIONAL QUESTIONS FOR FURTHER REFLECTION

How do you interpret the message you received?

*Can you use the oracle card's keyword in a sentence
to describe how you feel?*

*Does the card's message resonate with the question asked?
Why or why not? (Note that the answer can change when
you refer to this entry later.)*

What artwork, if any, on your selected card spoke to you?

✦ ✦ journal entry ✦ ✦

date _____ time _____

deck _____

QUESTION ASKED

_____

_____

card pulled _____

REFLECTION

_____

_____

_____

_____

_____

_____

_____

_____

_____

_____

_____

ADDITIONAL QUESTIONS FOR FURTHER REFLECTION

How do you interpret the message you received?

*Can you use the oracle card's keyword in a sentence
to describe how you feel?*

*Does the card's message resonate with the question asked?
Why or why not? (Note that the answer can change when
you refer to this entry later.)*

What artwork, if any, on your selected card spoke to you?

✦ ⋅ ⋅ journal entry ⋅ ⋅ ✦

date _____   time _____

deck _____

_____
_____

card pulled _____

REFLECTION

_____
_____
_____
_____
_____
_____
_____
_____
_____
_____
_____
_____

ADDITIONAL QUESTIONS FOR FURTHER REFLECTION

How do you interpret the message you received?

*Can you use the oracle card's keyword in a sentence
to describe how you feel?*

*Does the card's message resonate with the question asked?
Why or why not? (Note that the answer can change when
you refer to this entry later.)*

What artwork, if any, on your selected card spoke to you?

journal entry

date _____ time _____

deck _____

_____
_____

card pulled _____

REFLECTION

_____
_____
_____
_____
_____
_____
_____
_____
_____
_____
_____

ADDITIONAL QUESTIONS FOR FURTHER REFLECTION

How do you interpret the message you received?

*Can you use the oracle card's keyword in a sentence
to describe how you feel?*

*Does the card's message resonate with the question asked?
Why or why not? (Note that the answer can change when
you refer to this entry later.)*

What artwork, if any, on your selected card spoke to you?

✦ ·· journal entry ·· ✦

date _____ time _____

deck _____

QUESTION ASKED

_____

_____

card pulled _____

REFLECTION

_____

_____

_____

_____

_____

_____

_____

_____

_____

_____

_____

ADDITIONAL QUESTIONS FOR FURTHER REFLECTION

How do you interpret the message you received?

*Can you use the oracle card's keyword in a sentence
to describe how you feel?*

*Does the card's message resonate with the question asked?
Why or why not? (Note that the answer can change when
you refer to this entry later.)*

What artwork, if any, on your selected card spoke to you?

✦ journal entry ✦

date _____ time _____

deck _____

_____

_____

card pulled _____

REFLECTION

_____

_____

_____

_____

_____

_____

_____

_____

_____

_____

ADDITIONAL QUESTIONS FOR FURTHER REFLECTION

How do you interpret the message you received?

*Can you use the oracle card's keyword in a sentence
to describe how you feel?*

*Does the card's message resonate with the question asked?
Why or why not? (Note that the answer can change when
you refer to this entry later.)*

What artwork, if any, on your selected card spoke to you?

✦ ·· journal entry ·· ✦

date _____   time _____

deck _____

_____
_____

card pulled _____

REFLECTION

_____
_____
_____
_____
_____
_____
_____
_____
_____
_____
_____
_____

ADDITIONAL QUESTIONS FOR FURTHER REFLECTION

How do you interpret the message you received?

*Can you use the oracle card's keyword in a sentence
to describe how you feel?*

*Does the card's message resonate with the question asked?
Why or why not? (Note that the answer can change when
you refer to this entry later.)*

What artwork, if any, on your selected card spoke to you?

✦ • • journal entry • • ✦

date _____   time _____

deck _____

QUESTION ASKED

_____

_____

card pulled _____

REFLECTION

_____

_____

_____

_____

_____

_____

_____

_____

_____

_____

_____

ADDITIONAL QUESTIONS FOR FURTHER REFLECTION

How do you interpret the message you received?

*Can you use the oracle card's keyword in a sentence
to describe how you feel?*

*Does the card's message resonate with the question asked?
Why or why not? (Note that the answer can change when
you refer to this entry later.)*

What artwork, if any, on your selected card spoke to you?

✦ journal entry ✦

date _____ time _____

deck _____

QUESTION ASKED

_____
_____

card pulled _____

REFLECTION

_____
_____
_____
_____
_____
_____
_____
_____
_____
_____
_____

ADDITIONAL QUESTIONS FOR FURTHER REFLECTION

How do you interpret the message you received?

Can you use the oracle card's keyword in a sentence to describe how you feel?

Does the card's message resonate with the question asked? Why or why not? (Note that the answer can change when you refer to this entry later.)

What artwork, if any, on your selected card spoke to you?

✦ ✦ journal entry ✦ ✦

date _____   time _____

deck _____

QUESTION ASKED

_____

_____

card pulled _____

REFLECTION

_____

_____

_____

_____

_____

_____

_____

_____

_____

_____

_____

ADDITIONAL QUESTIONS FOR FURTHER REFLECTION

How do you interpret the message you received?

*Can you use the oracle card's keyword in a sentence
to describe how you feel?*

*Does the card's message resonate with the question asked?
Why or why not? (Note that the answer can change when
you refer to this entry later.)*

What artwork, if any, on your selected card spoke to you?

✦ ⋯ journal entry ⋯ ✦

date _____   time _____

deck _____

QUESTION ASKED

_____
_____

card pulled _____

REFLECTION

_____
_____
_____
_____
_____
_____
_____
_____
_____
_____
_____
_____

ADDITIONAL QUESTIONS FOR FURTHER REFLECTION

How do you interpret the message you received?

Can you use the oracle card's keyword in a sentence to describe how you feel?

Does the card's message resonate with the question asked? Why or why not? (Note that the answer can change when you refer to this entry later.)

What artwork, if any, on your selected card spoke to you?

✦•• journal entry ••✦

date _____   time _____

deck _____

QUESTION ASKED

_____

_____

card pulled _____

REFLECTION

_____

_____

_____

_____

_____

_____

_____

_____

_____

_____

_____

ADDITIONAL QUESTIONS FOR FURTHER REFLECTION

How do you interpret the message you received?

*Can you use the oracle card's keyword in a sentence
to describe how you feel?*

*Does the card's message resonate with the question asked?
Why or why not? (Note that the answer can change when
you refer to this entry later.)*

What artwork, if any, on your selected card spoke to you?

✦ ·· journal entry ·· ✦

date _____ time _____

deck _____

_____
_____

card pulled _____

REFLECTION

_____
_____
_____
_____
_____
_____
_____
_____
_____
_____
_____

ADDITIONAL QUESTIONS FOR FURTHER REFLECTION

How do you interpret the message you received?

*Can you use the oracle card's keyword in a sentence
to describe how you feel?*

*Does the card's message resonate with the question asked?
Why or why not? (Note that the answer can change when
you refer to this entry later.)*

What artwork, if any, on your selected card spoke to you?

✦ ·· journal entry ·· ✦

date _____   time _____

deck _____

_____

_____

card pulled _____

REFLECTION

_____
_____
_____
_____
_____
_____
_____
_____
_____
_____
_____

ADDITIONAL QUESTIONS FOR FURTHER REFLECTION

How do you interpret the message you received?

*Can you use the oracle card's keyword in a sentence
to describe how you feel?*

*Does the card's message resonate with the question asked?
Why or why not? (Note that the answer can change when
you refer to this entry later.)*

What artwork, if any, on your selected card spoke to you?

✦ ·· journal entry ·· ✦

date _____ time _____

deck _____

_____
_____

card pulled _____

REFLECTION

_____
_____
_____
_____
_____
_____
_____
_____
_____
_____

ADDITIONAL QUESTIONS FOR FURTHER REFLECTION

How do you interpret the message you received?

*Can you use the oracle card's keyword in a sentence
to describe how you feel?*

*Does the card's message resonate with the question asked?
Why or why not? (Note that the answer can change when
you refer to this entry later.)*

What artwork, if any, on your selected card spoke to you?

✦ • • journal entry • • ✦

date _____ time _____

deck _____

_____

_____

card pulled _____

REFLECTION

_____

_____

_____

_____

_____

_____

_____

_____

_____

_____

_____

ADDITIONAL QUESTIONS FOR FURTHER REFLECTION

How do you interpret the message you received?

*Can you use the oracle card's keyword in a sentence
to describe how you feel?*

*Does the card's message resonate with the question asked?
Why or why not? (Note that the answer can change when
you refer to this entry later.)*

What artwork, if any, on your selected card spoke to you?

✦ ∙∙ journal entry ∙∙ ✦

date _____ time _____

deck _____

QUESTION ASKED

_____
_____

card pulled _____

REFLECTION

_____
_____
_____
_____
_____
_____
_____
_____
_____
_____
_____

ADDITIONAL QUESTIONS FOR FURTHER REFLECTION

How do you interpret the message you received?

*Can you use the oracle card's keyword in a sentence
to describe how you feel?*

*Does the card's message resonate with the question asked?
Why or why not? (Note that the answer can change when
you refer to this entry later.)*

What artwork, if any, on your selected card spoke to you?

✦ · · journal entry · · ✦

date _____   time _____

deck _____

_____

_____

card pulled _____

REFLECTION

_____

_____

_____

_____

_____

_____

_____

_____

_____

_____

_____

ADDITIONAL QUESTIONS FOR FURTHER REFLECTION

How do you interpret the message you received?

*Can you use the oracle card's keyword in a sentence
to describe how you feel?*

*Does the card's message resonate with the question asked?
Why or why not? (Note that the answer can change when
you refer to this entry later.)*

What artwork, if any, on your selected card spoke to you?

◆ ◦ ◦ journal entry ◦ ◦ ◆

date _____   time _____

deck _____

_____

_____

card pulled _____

REFLECTION

_____

_____

_____

_____

_____

_____

_____

_____

_____

_____

_____

ADDITIONAL QUESTIONS FOR FURTHER REFLECTION

How do you interpret the message you received?

*Can you use the oracle card's keyword in a sentence
to describe how you feel?*

*Does the card's message resonate with the question asked?
Why or why not? (Note that the answer can change when
you refer to this entry later.)*

What artwork, if any, on your selected card spoke to you?

journal entry

date _____ time _____

deck _____

QUESTION ASKED

_____

_____

card pulled _____

REFLECTION

_____

_____

_____

_____

_____

_____

_____

_____

_____

_____

ADDITIONAL QUESTIONS FOR FURTHER REFLECTION

How do you interpret the message you received?

*Can you use the oracle card's keyword in a sentence
to describe how you feel?*

*Does the card's message resonate with the question asked?
Why or why not? (Note that the answer can change when
you refer to this entry later.)*

What artwork, if any, on your selected card spoke to you?

journal entry

date _____   time _____

deck _____

_____

_____

card pulled _____

REFLECTION

_____

_____

_____

_____

_____

_____

_____

_____

_____

_____

ADDITIONAL QUESTIONS FOR FURTHER REFLECTION

How do you interpret the message you received?

*Can you use the oracle card's keyword in a sentence
to describe how you feel?*

*Does the card's message resonate with the question asked?
Why or why not? (Note that the answer can change when
you refer to this entry later.)*

What artwork, if any, on your selected card spoke to you?

✦ • journal entry • ✦

date _____ time _____

deck _____

QUESTION ASKED

_____

_____

card pulled _____

REFLECTION

_____

_____

_____

_____

_____

_____

_____

_____

_____

ADDITIONAL QUESTIONS FOR FURTHER REFLECTION

How do you interpret the message you received?

*Can you use the oracle card's keyword in a sentence
to describe how you feel?*

*Does the card's message resonate with the question asked?
Why or why not? (Note that the answer can change when
you refer to this entry later.)*

What artwork, if any, on your selected card spoke to you?

journal entry

date _____ time _____

deck _____

_____

_____

card pulled _____

REFLECTION

_____

_____

_____

_____

_____

_____

_____

_____

_____

_____

_____

ADDITIONAL QUESTIONS FOR FURTHER REFLECTION

How do you interpret the message you received?

*Can you use the oracle card's keyword in a sentence
to describe how you feel?*

*Does the card's message resonate with the question asked?
Why or why not? (Note that the answer can change when
you refer to this entry later.)*

What artwork, if any, on your selected card spoke to you?

✦ · · journal entry · · ✦

date _____ time _____

deck _____

QUESTION ASKED

_____

_____

card pulled _____

REFLECTION

_____

_____

_____

_____

_____

_____

_____

_____

_____

_____

_____

ADDITIONAL QUESTIONS FOR FURTHER REFLECTION

How do you interpret the message you received?

*Can you use the oracle card's keyword in a sentence
to describe how you feel?*

*Does the card's message resonate with the question asked?
Why or why not? (Note that the answer can change when
you refer to this entry later.)*

What artwork, if any, on your selected card spoke to you?

✦ ·· journal entry ·· ✦

date _____ time _____

deck _____

QUESTION ASKED
_____

_____

card pulled _____

REFLECTION
_____

_____

_____

_____

_____

_____

_____

_____

_____

_____

ADDITIONAL QUESTIONS FOR FURTHER REFLECTION

How do you interpret the message you received?

*Can you use the oracle card's keyword in a sentence
to describe how you feel?*

*Does the card's message resonate with the question asked?
Why or why not? (Note that the answer can change when
you refer to this entry later.)*

What artwork, if any, on your selected card spoke to you?

✦ · · journal entry · · ✦

date _____ time _____

deck _____

_____

_____

card pulled _____

REFLECTION

_____

_____

_____

_____

_____

_____

_____

_____

_____

_____

_____

ADDITIONAL QUESTIONS FOR FURTHER REFLECTION

How do you interpret the message you received?

*Can you use the oracle card's keyword in a sentence
to describe how you feel?*

*Does the card's message resonate with the question asked?
Why or why not? (Note that the answer can change when
you refer to this entry later.)*

What artwork, if any, on your selected card spoke to you?

✦ • • journal entry • • ✦

date _____   time _____

deck _____

_____

_____

card pulled _____

REFLECTION

_____

_____

_____

_____

_____

_____

_____

_____

_____

_____

_____

ADDITIONAL QUESTIONS FOR FURTHER REFLECTION

How do you interpret the message you received?

*Can you use the oracle card's keyword in a sentence
to describe how you feel?*

*Does the card's message resonate with the question asked?
Why or why not? (Note that the answer can change when
you refer to this entry later.)*

What artwork, if any, on your selected card spoke to you?

✦ · journal entry · ✦

date _____   time _____
deck _____

_____
_____

card pulled _____

REFLECTION

_____
_____
_____
_____
_____
_____
_____
_____
_____
_____
_____
_____

ADDITIONAL QUESTIONS FOR FURTHER REFLECTION

How do you interpret the message you received?

*Can you use the oracle card's keyword in a sentence
to describe how you feel?*

*Does the card's message resonate with the question asked?
Why or why not? (Note that the answer can change when
you refer to this entry later.)*

What artwork, if any, on your selected card spoke to you?

✦ journal entry ✦

date _____   time _____
deck _____

_____
_____

card pulled _____

REFLECTION

_____
_____
_____
_____
_____
_____
_____
_____
_____
_____
_____

ADDITIONAL QUESTIONS FOR FURTHER REFLECTION

How do you interpret the message you received?

*Can you use the oracle card's keyword in a sentence
to describe how you feel?*

*Does the card's message resonate with the question asked?
Why or why not? (Note that the answer can change when
you refer to this entry later.)*

What artwork, if any, on your selected card spoke to you?

✦ ·· journal entry ·· ✦

date _____   time _____
deck _____

QUESTION ASKED

_____

_____

card pulled _____

REFLECTION

_____
_____
_____
_____
_____
_____
_____
_____
_____
_____
_____

ADDITIONAL QUESTIONS FOR FURTHER REFLECTION

How do you interpret the message you received?

*Can you use the oracle card's keyword in a sentence
to describe how you feel?*

*Does the card's message resonate with the question asked?
Why or why not? (Note that the answer can change when
you refer to this entry later.)*

What artwork, if any, on your selected card spoke to you?

✦ ·· journal entry ·· ✦

date _____ time _____

deck _____

QUESTION ASKED

_____

_____

card pulled _____

REFLECTION

_____

_____

_____

_____

_____

_____

_____

_____

_____

_____

_____

ADDITIONAL QUESTIONS FOR FURTHER REFLECTION

How do you interpret the message you received?

Can you use the oracle card's keyword in a sentence to describe how you feel?

Does the card's message resonate with the question asked? Why or why not? (Note that the answer can change when you refer to this entry later.)

What artwork, if any, on your selected card spoke to you?

✦ ·· journal entry ·· ✦

date _____   time _____

deck _____

_____

_____

card pulled _____

REFLECTION

_____

_____

_____

_____

_____

_____

_____

_____

_____

ADDITIONAL QUESTIONS FOR FURTHER REFLECTION

How do you interpret the message you received?

*Can you use the oracle card's keyword in a sentence
to describe how you feel?*

*Does the card's message resonate with the question asked?
Why or why not? (Note that the answer can change when
you refer to this entry later.)*

What artwork, if any, on your selected card spoke to you?

✦ ·· journal entry ·· ✦

date _____ time _____

deck _____

QUESTION ASKED

_____

_____

card pulled _____

REFLECTION

_____

_____

_____

_____

_____

_____

_____

_____

_____

_____

_____

ADDITIONAL QUESTIONS FOR FURTHER REFLECTION

How do you interpret the message you received?

*Can you use the oracle card's keyword in a sentence
to describe how you feel?*

*Does the card's message resonate with the question asked?
Why or why not? (Note that the answer can change when
you refer to this entry later.)*

What artwork, if any, on your selected card spoke to you?

journal entry

date _____ time _____

deck _____

_____

_____

card pulled _____

REFLECTION

_____

_____

_____

_____

_____

_____

_____

_____

_____

_____

_____

ADDITIONAL QUESTIONS FOR FURTHER REFLECTION

How do you interpret the message you received?

*Can you use the oracle card's keyword in a sentence
to describe how you feel?*

*Does the card's message resonate with the question asked?
Why or why not? (Note that the answer can change when
you refer to this entry later.)*

What artwork, if any, on your selected card spoke to you?

✦ ✦ journal entry ✦ ✦

date _____   time _____

deck _____

_____

_____

card pulled _____

REFLECTION

_____

_____

_____

_____

_____

_____

_____

_____

_____

_____

_____

ADDITIONAL QUESTIONS FOR FURTHER REFLECTION

How do you interpret the message you received?

*Can you use the oracle card's keyword in a sentence
to describe how you feel?*

*Does the card's message resonate with the question asked?
Why or why not? (Note that the answer can change when
you refer to this entry later.)*

What artwork, if any, on your selected card spoke to you?

✦ • • journal entry • • ✦

date _____ time _____

deck _____

QUESTION ASKED

_____

_____

card pulled _____

REFLECTION

_____

_____

_____

_____

_____

_____

_____

_____

_____

_____

_____

ADDITIONAL QUESTIONS FOR FURTHER REFLECTION

How do you interpret the message you received?

*Can you use the oracle card's keyword in a sentence
to describe how you feel?*

*Does the card's message resonate with the question asked?
Why or why not? (Note that the answer can change when
you refer to this entry later.)*

What artwork, if any, on your selected card spoke to you?

✦ ⋅ ✦ journal entry ✦ ⋅ ✦

date _____ time _____

deck _____

QUESTION ASKED

_____
_____

card pulled _____

REFLECTION

_____
_____
_____
_____
_____
_____
_____
_____
_____
_____
_____

ADDITIONAL QUESTIONS FOR FURTHER REFLECTION

How do you interpret the message you received?

*Can you use the oracle card's keyword in a sentence
to describe how you feel?*

*Does the card's message resonate with the question asked?
Why or why not? (Note that the answer can change when
you refer to this entry later.)*

What artwork, if any, on your selected card spoke to you?

✦ • ✦ journal entry ✦ • ✦

date _____   time _____

deck _____

_____

_____

card pulled _____

REFLECTION

_____

_____

_____

_____

_____

_____

_____

_____

_____

_____

_____

ADDITIONAL QUESTIONS FOR FURTHER REFLECTION

How do you interpret the message you received?

*Can you use the oracle card's keyword in a sentence
to describe how you feel?*

*Does the card's message resonate with the question asked?
Why or why not? (Note that the answer can change when
you refer to this entry later.)*

What artwork, if any, on your selected card spoke to you?

✦ ·· journal entry ·· ✦

date _____ time _____

deck _____

QUESTION ASKED

_____

_____

card pulled _____

REFLECTION

_____

_____

_____

_____

_____

_____

_____

_____

_____

_____

_____

ADDITIONAL QUESTIONS FOR FURTHER REFLECTION

How do you interpret the message you received?

*Can you use the oracle card's keyword in a sentence
to describe how you feel?*

*Does the card's message resonate with the question asked?
Why or why not? (Note that the answer can change when
you refer to this entry later.)*

What artwork, if any, on your selected card spoke to you?

✦ journal entry ✦

date _____   time _____

deck _____

_____

_____

card pulled _____

REFLECTION

_____

_____

_____

_____

_____

_____

_____

_____

_____

_____

_____

_____

ADDITIONAL QUESTIONS FOR FURTHER REFLECTION

How do you interpret the message you received?

*Can you use the oracle card's keyword in a sentence
to describe how you feel?*

*Does the card's message resonate with the question asked?
Why or why not? (Note that the answer can change when
you refer to this entry later.)*

What artwork, if any, on your selected card spoke to you?

✦ •• **journal entry** •• ✦

date _____   time _____

deck _____

_____

_____

card pulled _____

REFLECTION

_____

_____

_____

_____

_____

_____

_____

_____

_____

_____

_____

_____

ADDITIONAL QUESTIONS FOR FURTHER REFLECTION

How do you interpret the message you received?

*Can you use the oracle card's keyword in a sentence
to describe how you feel?*

*Does the card's message resonate with the question asked?
Why or why not? (Note that the answer can change when
you refer to this entry later.)*

What artwork, if any, on your selected card spoke to you?

journal entry

date _____   time _____
deck _____

QUESTION ASKED

_____

_____

card pulled _____

REFLECTION

_____

_____

_____

_____

_____

_____

_____

_____

_____

_____

ADDITIONAL QUESTIONS FOR FURTHER REFLECTION

How do you interpret the message you received?

*Can you use the oracle card's keyword in a sentence
to describe how you feel?*

*Does the card's message resonate with the question asked?
Why or why not? (Note that the answer can change when
you refer to this entry later.)*

What artwork, if any, on your selected card spoke to you?

✦ ⋅ ⋅ journal entry ⋅ ⋅ ✦

date _____ time _____

deck _____

QUESTION ASKED

_____

_____

card pulled _____

REFLECTION

_____

_____

_____

_____

_____

_____

_____

_____

_____

_____

_____

ADDITIONAL QUESTIONS FOR FURTHER REFLECTION

How do you interpret the message you received?

*Can you use the oracle card's keyword in a sentence
to describe how you feel?*

*Does the card's message resonate with the question asked?
Why or why not? (Note that the answer can change when
you refer to this entry later.)*

What artwork, if any, on your selected card spoke to you?

✦ · · journal entry · · ✦

date _____   time _____

deck _____

QUESTION ASKED

_____

_____

_____

card pulled _____

REFLECTION

_____

_____

_____

_____

_____

_____

_____

_____

_____

_____

ADDITIONAL QUESTIONS FOR FURTHER REFLECTION

How do you interpret the message you received?

*Can you use the oracle card's keyword in a sentence
to describe how you feel?*

*Does the card's message resonate with the question asked?
Why or why not? (Note that the answer can change when
you refer to this entry later.)*

What artwork, if any, on your selected card spoke to you?

✦ ∙∙ journal entry ∙∙ ✦

date _____ time _____

deck _____

QUESTION ASKED

....

_____

card pulled _____

REFLECTION

_____
....
_____
_____
....
_____
_____
_____
....
_____
_____

ADDITIONAL QUESTIONS FOR FURTHER REFLECTION

How do you interpret the message you received?

*Can you use the oracle card's keyword in a sentence
to describe how you feel?*

*Does the card's message resonate with the question asked?
Why or why not? (Note that the answer can change when
you refer to this entry later.)*

What artwork, if any, on your selected card spoke to you?

✦ ∘ ∘ journal entry ∘ ∘ ✦

date _____ time _____

deck _____

QUESTION ASKED

_____
_____

card pulled _____

REFLECTION

_____
_____
_____
_____
_____
_____
_____
_____
_____
_____
_____

ADDITIONAL QUESTIONS FOR FURTHER REFLECTION

How do you interpret the message you received?

Can you use the oracle card's keyword in a sentence to describe how you feel?

Does the card's message resonate with the question asked? Why or why not? (Note that the answer can change when you refer to this entry later.)

What artwork, if any, on your selected card spoke to you?

✦ ·· journal entry ·· ✦

date _____ time _____

deck _____

QUESTION ASKED

_____
_____

card pulled _____

REFLECTION

_____
_____
_____
_____
_____
_____
_____
_____
_____
_____
_____

ADDITIONAL QUESTIONS FOR FURTHER REFLECTION

How do you interpret the message you received?

Can you use the oracle card's keyword in a sentence to describe how you feel?

Does the card's message resonate with the question asked? Why or why not? (Note that the answer can change when you refer to this entry later.)

What artwork, if any, on your selected card spoke to you?

✦ · · journal entry · · ✦

date _____ time _____

deck _____

QUESTION ASKED

_____
_____

card pulled _____

REFLECTION

_____
_____
_____
_____
_____
_____
_____
_____
_____
_____
_____

ADDITIONAL QUESTIONS FOR FURTHER REFLECTION

How do you interpret the message you received?

*Can you use the oracle card's keyword in a sentence
to describe how you feel?*

*Does the card's message resonate with the question asked?
Why or why not? (Note that the answer can change when
you refer to this entry later.)*

What artwork, if any, on your selected card spoke to you?

✦ ·· journal entry ·· ✦

date _____ time _____

deck _____

_____

_____

card pulled _____

REFLECTION

_____

_____

_____

_____

_____

_____

_____

_____

_____

_____

_____

ADDITIONAL QUESTIONS FOR FURTHER REFLECTION

How do you interpret the message you received?

*Can you use the oracle card's keyword in a sentence
to describe how you feel?*

*Does the card's message resonate with the question asked?
Why or why not? (Note that the answer can change when
you refer to this entry later.)*

What artwork, if any, on your selected card spoke to you?

✦ · · journal entry · · ✦

date _____   time _____

deck _____

QUESTION ASKED

_____
_____

card pulled _____

REFLECTION

_____
_____
_____
_____
_____
_____
_____
_____
_____
_____

ADDITIONAL QUESTIONS FOR FURTHER REFLECTION

How do you interpret the message you received?

*Can you use the oracle card's keyword in a sentence
to describe how you feel?*

*Does the card's message resonate with the question asked?
Why or why not? (Note that the answer can change when
you refer to this entry later.)*

What artwork, if any, on your selected card spoke to you?

✦ · · journal entry · · ✦

date _____   time _____

deck _____

_____

_____

card pulled _____

REFLECTION

_____

_____

_____

_____

_____

_____

_____

_____

_____

_____

_____

ADDITIONAL QUESTIONS FOR FURTHER REFLECTION

How do you interpret the message you received?

*Can you use the oracle card's keyword in a sentence
to describe how you feel?*

*Does the card's message resonate with the question asked?
Why or why not? (Note that the answer can change when
you refer to this entry later.)*

What artwork, if any, on your selected card spoke to you?

✦ journal entry ✦

date _____   time _____

deck _____

QUESTION ASKED

_____

_____

card pulled _____

REFLECTION

_____

_____

_____

_____

_____

_____

_____

_____

_____

_____

ADDITIONAL QUESTIONS FOR FURTHER REFLECTION

How do you interpret the message you received?

Can you use the oracle card's keyword in a sentence to describe how you feel?

Does the card's message resonate with the question asked? Why or why not? (Note that the answer can change when you refer to this entry later.)

What artwork, if any, on your selected card spoke to you?

✦ • • journal entry • • ✦

date _____ time _____

deck _____

QUESTION ASKED

_____
_____

card pulled _____

REFLECTION

_____
_____
_____
_____
_____
_____
_____
_____
_____
_____
_____

ADDITIONAL QUESTIONS FOR FURTHER REFLECTION

How do you interpret the message you received?

*Can you use the oracle card's keyword in a sentence
to describe how you feel?*

*Does the card's message resonate with the question asked?
Why or why not? (Note that the answer can change when
you refer to this entry later.)*

What artwork, if any, on your selected card spoke to you?

✦ ⋯ journal entry ⋯ ✦

date _____ time _____

deck _____

QUESTION ASKED

_____

_____

card pulled _____

REFLECTION

_____

_____

_____

_____

_____

_____

_____

_____

_____

_____

ADDITIONAL QUESTIONS FOR FURTHER REFLECTION

How do you interpret the message you received?

*Can you use the oracle card's keyword in a sentence
to describe how you feel?*

*Does the card's message resonate with the question asked?
Why or why not? (Note that the answer can change when
you refer to this entry later.)*

What artwork, if any, on your selected card spoke to you?

✦ ⋯ journal entry ⋯ ✦

date _____ time _____

deck _____

_____

_____

card pulled _____

REFLECTION

_____

_____

_____

_____

_____

_____

_____

_____

_____

_____

ADDITIONAL QUESTIONS FOR FURTHER REFLECTION

How do you interpret the message you received?

*Can you use the oracle card's keyword in a sentence
to describe how you feel?*

*Does the card's message resonate with the question asked?
Why or why not? (Note that the answer can change when
you refer to this entry later.)*

What artwork, if any, on your selected card spoke to you?

✦ journal entry ✦

date _____ time _____

deck _____

QUESTION ASKED

_____

_____

card pulled _____

REFLECTION

_____
_____
_____
_____
_____
_____
_____
_____
_____
_____

ADDITIONAL QUESTIONS FOR FURTHER REFLECTION

How do you interpret the message you received?

*Can you use the oracle card's keyword in a sentence
to describe how you feel?*

*Does the card's message resonate with the question asked?
Why or why not? (Note that the answer can change when
you refer to this entry later.)*

What artwork, if any, on your selected card spoke to you?

✦• journal entry •✦

date _____ time _____

deck _____

QUESTION ASKED

_____
_____

card pulled _____

REFLECTION

_____
_____
_____
_____
_____
_____
_____
_____
_____
_____

ADDITIONAL QUESTIONS FOR FURTHER REFLECTION

How do you interpret the message you received?

*Can you use the oracle card's keyword in a sentence
to describe how you feel?*

*Does the card's message resonate with the question asked?
Why or why not? (Note that the answer can change when
you refer to this entry later.)*

What artwork, if any, on your selected card spoke to you?

✦ ·· journal entry ·· ✦

date _____   time _____

deck _____

_____
_____

card pulled _____

REFLECTION

_____
_____
_____
_____
_____
_____
_____
_____
_____
_____
_____
_____

ADDITIONAL QUESTIONS FOR FURTHER REFLECTION

How do you interpret the message you received?

Can you use the oracle card's keyword in a sentence to describe how you feel?

Does the card's message resonate with the question asked? Why or why not? (Note that the answer can change when you refer to this entry later.)

What artwork, if any, on your selected card spoke to you?

✦ · · journal entry · · ✦

date _____ time _____

deck _____

_____

_____

card pulled _____

REFLECTION

_____

_____

_____

_____

_____

_____

_____

_____

_____

_____

_____

ADDITIONAL QUESTIONS FOR FURTHER REFLECTION

How do you interpret the message you received?

*Can you use the oracle card's keyword in a sentence
to describe how you feel?*

*Does the card's message resonate with the question asked?
Why or why not? (Note that the answer can change when
you refer to this entry later.)*

What artwork, if any, on your selected card spoke to you?

✦ ·· journal entry ·· ✦

date _____   time _____

deck _____

QUESTION ASKED

_____

_____

card pulled _____

REFLECTION

_____

_____

_____

_____

_____

_____

_____

_____

_____

_____

ADDITIONAL QUESTIONS FOR FURTHER REFLECTION

How do you interpret the message you received?

*Can you use the oracle card's keyword in a sentence
to describe how you feel?*

*Does the card's message resonate with the question asked?
Why or why not? (Note that the answer can change when
you refer to this entry later.)*

What artwork, if any, on your selected card spoke to you?

✦ ·· journal entry ·· ✦

date _____ time _____

deck _____

QUESTION ASKED

_____
_____

card pulled _____

REFLECTION

_____
_____
_____
_____
_____
_____
_____
_____
_____
_____
_____

ADDITIONAL QUESTIONS FOR FURTHER REFLECTION

How do you interpret the message you received?

*Can you use the oracle card's keyword in a sentence
to describe how you feel?*

*Does the card's message resonate with the question asked?
Why or why not? (Note that the answer can change when
you refer to this entry later.)*

What artwork, if any, on your selected card spoke to you?

✦ • • journal entry • • ✦

date _____ time _____

deck _____

_____

_____

card pulled _____

REFLECTION

_____

_____

_____

_____

_____

_____

_____

_____

_____

_____

ADDITIONAL QUESTIONS FOR FURTHER REFLECTION

How do you interpret the message you received?

*Can you use the oracle card's keyword in a sentence
to describe how you feel?*

*Does the card's message resonate with the question asked?
Why or why not? (Note that the answer can change when
you refer to this entry later.)*

What artwork, if any, on your selected card spoke to you?

✦ ·· journal entry ·· ✦

date _____   time _____

deck _____

_____
_____

card pulled _____

REFLECTION

_____
_____
_____
_____
_____
_____
_____
_____
_____
_____
_____

ADDITIONAL QUESTIONS FOR FURTHER REFLECTION

How do you interpret the message you received?

Can you use the oracle card's keyword in a sentence to describe how you feel?

Does the card's message resonate with the question asked? Why or why not? (Note that the answer can change when you refer to this entry later.)

What artwork, if any, on your selected card spoke to you?

✦ ·· journal entry ·· ✦

date _____   time _____

deck _____

_____

_____

card pulled _____

REFLECTION

_____

_____

_____

_____

_____

_____

_____

_____

_____

_____

ADDITIONAL QUESTIONS FOR FURTHER REFLECTION

How do you interpret the message you received?

*Can you use the oracle card's keyword in a sentence
to describe how you feel?*

*Does the card's message resonate with the question asked?
Why or why not? (Note that the answer can change when
you refer to this entry later.)*

What artwork, if any, on your selected card spoke to you?

✦ ·· journal entry ·· ✦

date _____ time _____

deck _____

QUESTION ASKED

_____
_____

card pulled _____

REFLECTION

_____
_____
_____
_____
_____
_____
_____
_____
_____
_____

ADDITIONAL QUESTIONS FOR FURTHER REFLECTION

How do you interpret the message you received?

*Can you use the oracle card's keyword in a sentence
to describe how you feel?*

*Does the card's message resonate with the question asked?
Why or why not? (Note that the answer can change when
you refer to this entry later.)*

What artwork, if any, on your selected card spoke to you?

✦ · · journal entry · · ✦

date _____   time _____

deck _____

_____

_____

card pulled _____

REFLECTION

_____

_____

_____

_____

_____

_____

_____

_____

_____

_____

ADDITIONAL QUESTIONS FOR FURTHER REFLECTION

How do you interpret the message you received?

*Can you use the oracle card's keyword in a sentence
to describe how you feel?*

*Does the card's message resonate with the question asked?
Why or why not? (Note that the answer can change when
you refer to this entry later.)*

What artwork, if any, on your selected card spoke to you?

✦ ·· journal entry ·· ✦

date _____ time _____

deck _____

QUESTION ASKED

_____
_____

card pulled _____

REFLECTION

_____
_____
_____
_____
_____
_____
_____
_____
_____
_____
_____

ADDITIONAL QUESTIONS FOR FURTHER REFLECTION

How do you interpret the message you received?

*Can you use the oracle card's keyword in a sentence
to describe how you feel?*

*Does the card's message resonate with the question asked?
Why or why not? (Note that the answer can change when
you refer to this entry later.)*

What artwork, if any, on your selected card spoke to you?

✦ ·· journal entry ·· ✦

date _____   time _____

deck _____

QUESTION ASKED

_____

_____

card pulled _____

REFLECTION

_____

_____

_____

_____

_____

_____

_____

_____

_____

_____

_____

ADDITIONAL QUESTIONS FOR FURTHER REFLECTION

How do you interpret the message you received?

*Can you use the oracle card's keyword in a sentence
to describe how you feel?*

*Does the card's message resonate with the question asked?
Why or why not? (Note that the answer can change when
you refer to this entry later.)*

What artwork, if any, on your selected card spoke to you?

✦ · · journal entry · · ✦

date _____ time _____

deck _____

_____

_____

card pulled _____

_____

_____

_____

_____

_____

_____

_____

_____

_____

_____

_____

ADDITIONAL QUESTIONS FOR FURTHER REFLECTION

How do you interpret the message you received?

*Can you use the oracle card's keyword in a sentence
to describe how you feel?*

*Does the card's message resonate with the question asked?
Why or why not? (Note that the answer can change when
you refer to this entry later.)*

What artwork, if any, on your selected card spoke to you?

✦ ∙∙ journal entry ∙∙ ✦

date _____ time _____

deck _____

QUESTION ASKED

_____

_____

card pulled _____

REFLECTION

_____

_____

_____

_____

_____

_____

_____

_____

_____

_____

_____

ADDITIONAL QUESTIONS FOR FURTHER REFLECTION

How do you interpret the message you received?

*Can you use the oracle card's keyword in a sentence
to describe how you feel?*

*Does the card's message resonate with the question asked?
Why or why not? (Note that the answer can change when
you refer to this entry later.)*

What artwork, if any, on your selected card spoke to you?

✦ ✦ journal entry ✦ ✦

date _____   time _____

deck _____

QUESTION ASKED

_____
_____

card pulled _____

REFLECTION

_____
_____
_____
_____
_____
_____
_____
_____
_____
_____

ADDITIONAL QUESTIONS FOR FURTHER REFLECTION

How do you interpret the message you received?

*Can you use the oracle card's keyword in a sentence
to describe how you feel?*

*Does the card's message resonate with the question asked?
Why or why not? (Note that the answer can change when
you refer to this entry later.)*

What artwork, if any, on your selected card spoke to you?

✦ ·· journal entry ·· ✦

date _____   time _____

deck _____

QUESTION ASKED

_____
_____

card pulled _____

REFLECTION

_____
_____
_____
_____
_____
_____
_____
_____
_____
_____
_____

ADDITIONAL QUESTIONS FOR FURTHER REFLECTION

How do you interpret the message you received?

*Can you use the oracle card's keyword in a sentence
to describe how you feel?*

*Does the card's message resonate with the question asked?
Why or why not? (Note that the answer can change when
you refer to this entry later.)*

What artwork, if any, on your selected card spoke to you?

✦ ✦ journal entry ✦ ✦

date _____ time _____

deck _____

_____

_____

card pulled _____

REFLECTION

_____

_____

_____

_____

_____

_____

_____

_____

_____

_____

ADDITIONAL QUESTIONS FOR FURTHER REFLECTION

How do you interpret the message you received?

*Can you use the oracle card's keyword in a sentence
to describe how you feel?*

*Does the card's message resonate with the question asked?
Why or why not? (Note that the answer can change when
you refer to this entry later.)*

What artwork, if any, on your selected card spoke to you?

✦ ·✦ journal entry ✦· ✦

date _____ time _____

deck _____

_____

_____

card pulled _____

REFLECTION

_____

_____

_____

_____

_____

_____

_____

_____

_____

_____

_____

ADDITIONAL QUESTIONS FOR FURTHER REFLECTION

How do you interpret the message you received?

Can you use the oracle card's keyword in a sentence to describe how you feel?

Does the card's message resonate with the question asked? Why or why not? (Note that the answer can change when you refer to this entry later.)

What artwork, if any, on your selected card spoke to you?

✦ ·· journal entry ·· ✦

date _____ time _____

deck _____

_____

_____

card pulled _____

REFLECTION

_____

_____

_____

_____

_____

_____

_____

_____

_____

_____

ADDITIONAL QUESTIONS FOR FURTHER REFLECTION

How do you interpret the message you received?

*Can you use the oracle card's keyword in a sentence
to describe how you feel?*

*Does the card's message resonate with the question asked?
Why or why not? (Note that the answer can change when
you refer to this entry later.)*

What artwork, if any, on your selected card spoke to you?

✦ ·· journal entry ·· ✦

date _____ time _____

deck _____

_____

_____

card pulled _____

REFLECTION

_____

_____

_____

_____

_____

_____

_____

_____

_____

_____

ADDITIONAL QUESTIONS FOR FURTHER REFLECTION

How do you interpret the message you received?

*Can you use the oracle card's keyword in a sentence
to describe how you feel?*

*Does the card's message resonate with the question asked?
Why or why not? (Note that the answer can change when
you refer to this entry later.)*

What artwork, if any, on your selected card spoke to you?

✦ ·· journal entry ·· ✦

date _____ time _____

deck _____

QUESTION ASKED

_____
_____

card pulled _____

REFLECTION

_____
_____
_____
_____
_____
_____
_____
_____
_____
_____
_____

ADDITIONAL QUESTIONS FOR FURTHER REFLECTION

How do you interpret the message you received?

*Can you use the oracle card's keyword in a sentence
to describe how you feel?*

*Does the card's message resonate with the question asked?
Why or why not? (Note that the answer can change when
you refer to this entry later.)*

What artwork, if any, on your selected card spoke to you?

✦ ∙∙ journal entry ∙∙ ✦

date _____   time _____

deck _____

_____
_____

card pulled _____

_____
_____
_____
_____
_____
_____
_____
_____
_____
_____
_____

ADDITIONAL QUESTIONS FOR FURTHER REFLECTION

How do you interpret the message you received?

Can you use the oracle card's keyword in a sentence
to describe how you feel?

Does the card's message resonate with the question asked?
Why or why not? (Note that the answer can change when
you refer to this entry later.)

What artwork, if any, on your selected card spoke to you?

✦ ·· journal entry ·· ✦

date _____   time _____

deck _____

QUESTION ASKED

_____
_____

card pulled _____

REFLECTION

_____
_____
_____
_____
_____
_____
_____
_____
_____
_____
_____

ADDITIONAL QUESTIONS FOR FURTHER REFLECTION

How do you interpret the message you received?

*Can you use the oracle card's keyword in a sentence
to describe how you feel?*

*Does the card's message resonate with the question asked?
Why or why not? (Note that the answer can change when
you refer to this entry later.)*

What artwork, if any, on your selected card spoke to you?

✦ ·· journal entry ·· ✦

date _____   time _____

deck _____

QUESTION ASKED

_____
_____

card pulled _____

REFLECTION

_____
_____
_____
_____
_____
_____
_____
_____
_____
_____
_____

ADDITIONAL QUESTIONS FOR FURTHER REFLECTION

How do you interpret the message you received?

Can you use the oracle card's keyword in a sentence to describe how you feel?

Does the card's message resonate with the question asked? Why or why not? (Note that the answer can change when you refer to this entry later.)

What artwork, if any, on your selected card spoke to you?

✦·· journal entry ··✦

date _____   time _____

deck _____

QUESTION ASKED

_____

_____

card pulled _____

REFLECTION

_____

_____

_____

_____

_____

_____

_____

_____

_____

_____

_____

ADDITIONAL QUESTIONS FOR FURTHER REFLECTION

How do you interpret the message you received?

*Can you use the oracle card's keyword in a sentence
to describe how you feel?*

*Does the card's message resonate with the question asked?
Why or why not? (Note that the answer can change when
you refer to this entry later.)*

What artwork, if any, on your selected card spoke to you?

journal entry

date _____   time _____

deck _____

_____

_____

card pulled _____

REFLECTION

_____
_____
_____
_____
_____
_____
_____
_____
_____
_____
_____

ADDITIONAL QUESTIONS FOR FURTHER REFLECTION

How do you interpret the message you received?

*Can you use the oracle card's keyword in a sentence
to describe how you feel?*

*Does the card's message resonate with the question asked?
Why or why not? (Note that the answer can change when
you refer to this entry later.)*

What artwork, if any, on your selected card spoke to you?

✦ • • journal entry • • ✦

date _____ time _____

deck _____

QUESTION ASKED

_____
_____

card pulled _____

REFLECTION

_____
_____
_____
_____
_____
_____
_____
_____
_____
_____
_____

ADDITIONAL QUESTIONS FOR FURTHER REFLECTION

How do you interpret the message you received?

*Can you use the oracle card's keyword in a sentence
to describe how you feel?*

*Does the card's message resonate with the question asked?
Why or why not? (Note that the answer can change when
you refer to this entry later.)*

What artwork, if any, on your selected card spoke to you?

✦ ·· journal entry ·· ✦

date _____ time _____

deck _____

_____

_____

card pulled _____

REFLECTION

_____

_____

_____

_____

_____

_____

_____

_____

_____

_____

_____

ADDITIONAL QUESTIONS FOR FURTHER REFLECTION

How do you interpret the message you received?

*Can you use the oracle card's keyword in a sentence
to describe how you feel?*

*Does the card's message resonate with the question asked?
Why or why not? (Note that the answer can change when
you refer to this entry later.)*

What artwork, if any, on your selected card spoke to you?

✦ ✦ journal entry ✦ ✦

date _____ time _____

deck _____

QUESTION ASKED

_____
_____

card pulled _____

REFLECTION

_____
_____
_____
_____
_____
_____
_____
_____
_____
_____
_____

ADDITIONAL QUESTIONS FOR FURTHER REFLECTION

How do you interpret the message you received?

Can you use the oracle card's keyword in a sentence to describe how you feel?

Does the card's message resonate with the question asked? Why or why not? (Note that the answer can change when you refer to this entry later.)

What artwork, if any, on your selected card spoke to you?

✦ ·· journal entry ·· ✦

date _____   time _____

deck _____

_____

_____

card pulled _____

REFLECTION

_____
_____
_____
_____
_____
_____
_____
_____
_____
_____
_____

ADDITIONAL QUESTIONS FOR FURTHER REFLECTION

How do you interpret the message you received?

*Can you use the oracle card's keyword in a sentence
to describe how you feel?*

*Does the card's message resonate with the question asked?
Why or why not? (Note that the answer can change when
you refer to this entry later.)*

What artwork, if any, on your selected card spoke to you?

✦ •• journal entry •• ✦

date _____ time _____

deck _____

_____

_____

card pulled _____

REFLECTION

_____
_____
_____
_____
_____
_____
_____
_____
_____
_____
_____

ADDITIONAL QUESTIONS FOR FURTHER REFLECTION

How do you interpret the message you received?

Can you use the oracle card's keyword in a sentence to describe how you feel?

Does the card's message resonate with the question asked? Why or why not? (Note that the answer can change when you refer to this entry later.)

What artwork, if any, on your selected card spoke to you?

✦ •• journal entry •• ✦

date _____ time _____

deck _____

QUESTION ASKED

_____

_____

card pulled _____

REFLECTION

_____

_____

_____

_____

_____

_____

_____

_____

_____

_____

_____

ADDITIONAL QUESTIONS FOR FURTHER REFLECTION

How do you interpret the message you received?

*Can you use the oracle card's keyword in a sentence
to describe how you feel?*

*Does the card's message resonate with the question asked?
Why or why not? (Note that the answer can change when
you refer to this entry later.)*

What artwork, if any, on your selected card spoke to you?

✦ · · journal entry · · ✦

date _____ time _____

deck _____

_____

_____

card pulled _____

REFLECTION

_____

_____

_____

_____

_____

_____

_____

_____

_____

_____

_____

ADDITIONAL QUESTIONS FOR FURTHER REFLECTION

How do you interpret the message you received?

*Can you use the oracle card's keyword in a sentence
to describe how you feel?*

*Does the card's message resonate with the question asked?
Why or why not? (Note that the answer can change when
you refer to this entry later.)*

What artwork, if any, on your selected card spoke to you?

✦ ･ ･ journal entry ✦ ･ ✦

date _____   time _____

deck _____

QUESTION ASKED

_____

_____

card pulled _____

REFLECTION

_____

_____

_____

_____

_____

_____

_____

_____

_____

_____

_____

ADDITIONAL QUESTIONS FOR FURTHER REFLECTION

How do you interpret the message you received?

*Can you use the oracle card's keyword in a sentence
to describe how you feel?*

*Does the card's message resonate with the question asked?
Why or why not? (Note that the answer can change when
you refer to this entry later.)*

What artwork, if any, on your selected card spoke to you?

✦ ⋅ ⋅ journal entry ⋅ ⋅ ✦

date _____   time _____

deck _____

_____

_____

card pulled _____

REFLECTION

_____

_____

_____

_____

_____

_____

_____

_____

_____

_____

_____

_____

ADDITIONAL QUESTIONS FOR FURTHER REFLECTION

How do you interpret the message you received?

*Can you use the oracle card's keyword in a sentence
to describe how you feel?*

*Does the card's message resonate with the question asked?
Why or why not? (Note that the answer can change when
you refer to this entry later.)*

What artwork, if any, on your selected card spoke to you?

✦ ⋅⋅ journal entry ⋅⋅ ✦

date _____ time _____

deck _____

QUESTION ASKED

_____

_____

card pulled _____

REFLECTION

_____

_____

_____

_____

_____

_____

_____

_____

_____

_____

_____

_____

ADDITIONAL QUESTIONS FOR FURTHER REFLECTION

How do you interpret the message you received?

*Can you use the oracle card's keyword in a sentence
to describe how you feel?*

*Does the card's message resonate with the question asked?
Why or why not? (Note that the answer can change when
you refer to this entry later.)*

What artwork, if any, on your selected card spoke to you?

✦ ·· journal entry ·· ✦

date _____ time _____

deck _____

QUESTION ASKED

_____
_____

card pulled _____

REFLECTION

_____
_____
_____
_____
_____
_____
_____
_____
_____
_____
_____

ADDITIONAL QUESTIONS FOR FURTHER REFLECTION

How do you interpret the message you received?

*Can you use the oracle card's keyword in a sentence
to describe how you feel?*

*Does the card's message resonate with the question asked?
Why or why not? (Note that the answer can change when
you refer to this entry later.)*

What artwork, if any, on your selected card spoke to you?

✦ • • journal entry • • ✦

date _____   time _____

deck _____

_____

_____

card pulled _____

REFLECTION

_____

_____

_____

_____

_____

_____

_____

_____

_____

_____

ADDITIONAL QUESTIONS FOR FURTHER REFLECTION

How do you interpret the message you received?

*Can you use the oracle card's keyword in a sentence
to describe how you feel?*

*Does the card's message resonate with the question asked?
Why or why not? (Note that the answer can change when
you refer to this entry later.)*

What artwork, if any, on your selected card spoke to you?

◆ • • journal entry • • ◆

date _____   time _____

deck _____

QUESTION ASKED

_____

_____

card pulled _____

REFLECTION

_____

_____

_____

_____

_____

_____

_____

_____

_____

_____

_____

ADDITIONAL QUESTIONS FOR FURTHER REFLECTION

How do you interpret the message you received?

*Can you use the oracle card's keyword in a sentence
to describe how you feel?*

*Does the card's message resonate with the question asked?
Why or why not? (Note that the answer can change when
you refer to this entry later.)*

What artwork, if any, on your selected card spoke to you?

❖ ··· journal entry ··· ❖

date _____ time _____

deck _____

QUESTION ASKED

_____

_____

card pulled _____

REFLECTION

_____

_____

_____

_____

_____

_____

_____

_____

_____

_____

ADDITIONAL QUESTIONS FOR FURTHER REFLECTION

How do you interpret the message you received?

*Can you use the oracle card's keyword in a sentence
to describe how you feel?*

*Does the card's message resonate with the question asked?
Why or why not? (Note that the answer can change when
you refer to this entry later.)*

What artwork, if any, on your selected card spoke to you?

✦ ⋅ ⋅ journal entry ⋅ ✦

date _____   time _____

deck _____

_____

_____

card pulled _____

REFLECTION

_____

_____

_____

_____

_____

_____

_____

_____

_____

_____

ADDITIONAL QUESTIONS FOR FURTHER REFLECTION

How do you interpret the message you received?

*Can you use the oracle card's keyword in a sentence
to describe how you feel?*

*Does the card's message resonate with the question asked?
Why or why not? (Note that the answer can change when
you refer to this entry later.)*

What artwork, if any, on your selected card spoke to you?

✦ journal entry ✦

date _____ time _____

deck _____

QUESTION ASKED

_____

_____

card pulled _____

REFLECTION

_____

_____

_____

_____

_____

_____

_____

_____

_____

_____

_____

ADDITIONAL QUESTIONS FOR FURTHER REFLECTION

How do you interpret the message you received?

*Can you use the oracle card's keyword in a sentence
to describe how you feel?*

*Does the card's message resonate with the question asked?
Why or why not? (Note that the answer can change when
you refer to this entry later.)*

What artwork, if any, on your selected card spoke to you?

✦ • journal entry • ✦

date _____   time _____

deck _____

QUESTION ASKED

_____
_____
_____

card pulled _____

REFLECTION

_____
_____
_____
_____
_____
_____
_____
_____
_____
_____
_____
_____

ADDITIONAL QUESTIONS FOR FURTHER REFLECTION

How do you interpret the message you received?

*Can you use the oracle card's keyword in a sentence
to describe how you feel?*

*Does the card's message resonate with the question asked?
Why or why not? (Note that the answer can change when
you refer to this entry later.)*

What artwork, if any, on your selected card spoke to you?

✦ · · journal entry · · ✦

date _____   time _____

deck _____

QUESTION ASKED

_____

_____

card pulled _____

REFLECTION

_____

_____

_____

_____

_____

_____

_____

_____

_____

_____

_____

ADDITIONAL QUESTIONS FOR FURTHER REFLECTION

How do you interpret the message you received?

*Can you use the oracle card's keyword in a sentence
to describe how you feel?*

*Does the card's message resonate with the question asked?
Why or why not? (Note that the answer can change when
you refer to this entry later.)*

What artwork, if any, on your selected card spoke to you?

✦ · · journal entry · · ✦

date _____ time _____

deck _____

_____
_____
_____

card pulled _____

REFLECTION

_____
_____
_____
_____
_____
_____
_____
_____
_____
_____
_____

ADDITIONAL QUESTIONS FOR FURTHER REFLECTION

How do you interpret the message you received?

*Can you use the oracle card's keyword in a sentence
to describe how you feel?*

*Does the card's message resonate with the question asked?
Why or why not? (Note that the answer can change when
you refer to this entry later.)*

What artwork, if any, on your selected card spoke to you?

❖ ⋅ journal entry ⋅ ❖

date _____   time _____

deck _____

_____

_____

card pulled _____

REFLECTION

_____

_____

_____

_____

_____

_____

_____

_____

_____

_____

_____

ADDITIONAL QUESTIONS FOR FURTHER REFLECTION

How do you interpret the message you received?

*Can you use the oracle card's keyword in a sentence
to describe how you feel?*

*Does the card's message resonate with the question asked?
Why or why not? (Note that the answer can change when
you refer to this entry later.)*

What artwork, if any, on your selected card spoke to you?

✦ • • journal entry • • ✦

date _____   time _____

deck _____

....

....

card pulled _____

REFLECTION

....

....

....

....

....

....

....

....

....

....

ADDITIONAL QUESTIONS FOR FURTHER REFLECTION

How do you interpret the message you received?

Can you use the oracle card's keyword in a sentence to describe how you feel?

Does the card's message resonate with the question asked? Why or why not? (Note that the answer can change when you refer to this entry later.)

What artwork, if any, on your selected card spoke to you?

✦ ⋯ journal entry ⋯ ✦

date _____   time _____

deck _____

_____

_____

card pulled _____

REFLECTION

_____
_____
_____
_____
_____
_____
_____
_____
_____
_____
_____

ADDITIONAL QUESTIONS FOR FURTHER REFLECTION

How do you interpret the message you received?

*Can you use the oracle card's keyword in a sentence
to describe how you feel?*

*Does the card's message resonate with the question asked?
Why or why not? (Note that the answer can change when
you refer to this entry later.)*

What artwork, if any, on your selected card spoke to you?

✦ •✧• journal entry •✧• ✦

date _____   time _____

deck _____

_____

_____

card pulled _____

REFLECTION

_____

_____

_____

_____

_____

_____

_____

_____

_____

_____

ADDITIONAL QUESTIONS FOR FURTHER REFLECTION

How do you interpret the message you received?

*Can you use the oracle card's keyword in a sentence
to describe how you feel?*

*Does the card's message resonate with the question asked?
Why or why not? (Note that the answer can change when
you refer to this entry later.)*

What artwork, if any, on your selected card spoke to you?

✦ ⋅ ⋅ journal entry ⋅ ⋅ ✦

date _____   time _____

deck _____

_____

_____

card pulled _____

REFLECTION

_____

_____

_____

_____

_____

_____

_____

_____

_____

_____

_____

ADDITIONAL QUESTIONS FOR FURTHER REFLECTION

How do you interpret the message you received?

*Can you use the oracle card's keyword in a sentence
to describe how you feel?*

*Does the card's message resonate with the question asked?
Why or why not? (Note that the answer can change when
you refer to this entry later.)*

What artwork, if any, on your selected card spoke to you?

✦ ·· journal entry ·· ✦

date _____ time _____

deck _____

_____

_____

card pulled _____

REFLECTION

_____

_____

_____

_____

_____

_____

_____

_____

_____

_____

_____

ADDITIONAL QUESTIONS FOR FURTHER REFLECTION

How do you interpret the message you received?

*Can you use the oracle card's keyword in a sentence
to describe how you feel?*

*Does the card's message resonate with the question asked?
Why or why not? (Note that the answer can change when
you refer to this entry later.)*

What artwork, if any, on your selected card spoke to you?

✦ · · journal entry · · ✦

date _____   time _____

deck _____

QUESTION ASKED

_____

_____

card pulled _____

REFLECTION

_____

_____

_____

_____

_____

_____

_____

_____

_____

_____

_____

ADDITIONAL QUESTIONS FOR FURTHER REFLECTION

How do you interpret the message you received?

*Can you use the oracle card's keyword in a sentence
to describe how you feel?*

*Does the card's message resonate with the question asked?
Why or why not? (Note that the answer can change when
you refer to this entry later.)*

What artwork, if any, on your selected card spoke to you?

✦ ·· journal entry ·· ✦

date _____ time _____

deck _____

_____

_____

card pulled _____

REFLECTION

_____

_____

_____

_____

_____

_____

_____

_____

_____

_____

ADDITIONAL QUESTIONS FOR FURTHER REFLECTION

How do you interpret the message you received?

*Can you use the oracle card's keyword in a sentence
to describe how you feel?*

*Does the card's message resonate with the question asked?
Why or why not? (Note that the answer can change when
you refer to this entry later.)*

What artwork, if any, on your selected card spoke to you?

✦ ·· journal entry ·· ✦

date _____ time _____

deck _____

QUESTION ASKED

....
....

card pulled _____

REFLECTION

_____
_____
_____
_____
_____
_____
_____
_____
_____
_____

ADDITIONAL QUESTIONS FOR FURTHER REFLECTION

How do you interpret the message you received?

*Can you use the oracle card's keyword in a sentence
to describe how you feel?*

*Does the card's message resonate with the question asked?
Why or why not? (Note that the answer can change when
you refer to this entry later.)*

What artwork, if any, on your selected card spoke to you?

✦ ·· journal entry ·· ✦

date _____ time _____

deck _____

_____
_____

card pulled _____

REFLECTION

_____
_____
_____
_____
_____
_____
_____
_____
_____
_____
_____

ADDITIONAL QUESTIONS FOR FURTHER REFLECTION

How do you interpret the message you received?

*Can you use the oracle card's keyword in a sentence
to describe how you feel?*

*Does the card's message resonate with the question asked?
Why or why not? (Note that the answer can change when
you refer to this entry later.)*

What artwork, if any, on your selected card spoke to you?

✦ · · journal entry · · ✦

date _____   time _____

deck _____

QUESTION ASKED

_____

_____

card pulled _____

REFLECTION

_____

_____

_____

_____

_____

_____

_____

_____

_____

_____

_____

ADDITIONAL QUESTIONS FOR FURTHER REFLECTION

How do you interpret the message you received?

*Can you use the oracle card's keyword in a sentence
to describe how you feel?*

*Does the card's message resonate with the question asked?
Why or why not? (Note that the answer can change when
you refer to this entry later.)*

What artwork, if any, on your selected card spoke to you?

✦ • • journal entry • • ✦

date _____ time _____

deck _____

QUESTION ASKED

_____

_____

card pulled _____

REFLECTION

_____

_____

_____

_____

_____

_____

_____

_____

_____

_____

ADDITIONAL QUESTIONS FOR FURTHER REFLECTION

How do you interpret the message you received?

*Can you use the oracle card's keyword in a sentence
to describe how you feel?*

*Does the card's message resonate with the question asked?
Why or why not? (Note that the answer can change when
you refer to this entry later.)*

What artwork, if any, on your selected card spoke to you?

✦ ∙ ∙ journal entry ∙ ∙ ✦

date _____   time _____

deck _____

_____

_____

card pulled _____

REFLECTION

_____

_____

_____

_____

_____

_____

_____

_____

_____

_____

_____

ADDITIONAL QUESTIONS FOR FURTHER REFLECTION

How do you interpret the message you received?

*Can you use the oracle card's keyword in a sentence
to describe how you feel?*

*Does the card's message resonate with the question asked?
Why or why not? (Note that the answer can change when
you refer to this entry later.)*

What artwork, if any, on your selected card spoke to you?

✦ • • journal entry • • ✦

date _____   time _____

deck _____

_____

_____

card pulled _____

REFLECTION

_____

_____

_____

_____

_____

_____

_____

_____

_____

_____

_____

ADDITIONAL QUESTIONS FOR FURTHER REFLECTION

How do you interpret the message you received?

*Can you use the oracle card's keyword in a sentence
to describe how you feel?*

*Does the card's message resonate with the question asked?
Why or why not? (Note that the answer can change when
you refer to this entry later.)*

What artwork, if any, on your selected card spoke to you?

✦ • • journal entry • • ✦

date _____ time _____

deck _____

_____

_____

card pulled _____

REFLECTION

_____

_____

_____

_____

_____

_____

_____

_____

_____

_____

ADDITIONAL QUESTIONS FOR FURTHER REFLECTION

How do you interpret the message you received?

*Can you use the oracle card's keyword in a sentence
to describe how you feel?*

*Does the card's message resonate with the question asked?
Why or why not? (Note that the answer can change when
you refer to this entry later.)*

What artwork, if any, on your selected card spoke to you?

✦ • • journal entry • • ✦

date _____ time _____

deck _____

_____
_____

card pulled _____

REFLECTION

_____
_____
_____
_____
_____
_____
_____
_____
_____
_____
_____
_____

ADDITIONAL QUESTIONS FOR FURTHER REFLECTION

How do you interpret the message you received?

*Can you use the oracle card's keyword in a sentence
to describe how you feel?*

*Does the card's message resonate with the question asked?
Why or why not? (Note that the answer can change when
you refer to this entry later.)*

What artwork, if any, on your selected card spoke to you?

✦ • ✦ journal entry ✦ • ✦

date _____ time _____

deck _____

_____
_____

card pulled _____

REFLECTION

_____
_____
_____
_____
_____
_____
_____
_____
_____
_____
_____

ADDITIONAL QUESTIONS FOR FURTHER REFLECTION

How do you interpret the message you received?

*Can you use the oracle card's keyword in a sentence
to describe how you feel?*

*Does the card's message resonate with the question asked?
Why or why not? (Note that the answer can change when
you refer to this entry later.)*

What artwork, if any, on your selected card spoke to you?

✦ • • journal entry • • ✦

date _____ time _____

deck _____

QUESTION ASKED

_____

_____

card pulled _____

REFLECTION

_____

_____

_____

_____

_____

_____

_____

_____

_____

_____

_____

ADDITIONAL QUESTIONS FOR FURTHER REFLECTION

How do you interpret the message you received?

Can you use the oracle card's keyword in a sentence to describe how you feel?

Does the card's message resonate with the question asked? Why or why not? (Note that the answer can change when you refer to this entry later.)

What artwork, if any, on your selected card spoke to you?

✦ · journal entry · ✦

date _____ time _____

deck _____

QUESTION ASKED

_____

_____

card pulled _____

REFLECTION

_____

_____

_____

_____

_____

_____

_____

_____

_____

_____

_____

ADDITIONAL QUESTIONS FOR FURTHER REFLECTION

How do you interpret the message you received?

*Can you use the oracle card's keyword in a sentence
to describe how you feel?*

*Does the card's message resonate with the question asked?
Why or why not? (Note that the answer can change when
you refer to this entry later.)*

What artwork, if any, on your selected card spoke to you?

✦ ·· journal entry ·· ✦

date _____   time _____

deck _____

QUESTION ASKED

_____
_____

card pulled _____

REFLECTION

_____
_____
_____
_____
_____
_____
_____
_____
_____
_____
_____
_____
_____
_____

ADDITIONAL QUESTIONS FOR FURTHER REFLECTION

How do you interpret the message you received?

*Can you use the oracle card's keyword in a sentence
to describe how you feel?*

*Does the card's message resonate with the question asked?
Why or why not? (Note that the answer can change when
you refer to this entry later.)*

What artwork, if any, on your selected card spoke to you?

✦ ·· journal entry ·· ✦

date _____   time _____
deck _____

QUESTION ASKED

_____
_____

card pulled _____

REFLECTION

_____
_____
_____
_____
_____
_____
_____
_____
_____
_____
_____

ADDITIONAL QUESTIONS FOR FURTHER REFLECTION

How do you interpret the message you received?

*Can you use the oracle card's keyword in a sentence
to describe how you feel?*

*Does the card's message resonate with the question asked?
Why or why not? (Note that the answer can change when
you refer to this entry later.)*

What artwork, if any, on your selected card spoke to you?

✦ ⋅⋅ journal entry ⋅⋅ ✦

date _____   time _____

deck _____

_____

_____

card pulled _____

REFLECTION

_____

_____

_____

_____

_____

_____

_____

_____

_____

_____

_____

ADDITIONAL QUESTIONS FOR FURTHER REFLECTION

How do you interpret the message you received?

*Can you use the oracle card's keyword in a sentence
to describe how you feel?*

*Does the card's message resonate with the question asked?
Why or why not? (Note that the answer can change when
you refer to this entry later.)*

What artwork, if any, on your selected card spoke to you?

✦ ·· journal entry ·· ✦

date _____ time _____

deck _____

_____

_____

card pulled _____

REFLECTION

_____

_____

_____

_____

_____

_____

_____

_____

_____

_____

_____

ADDITIONAL QUESTIONS FOR FURTHER REFLECTION

How do you interpret the message you received?

*Can you use the oracle card's keyword in a sentence
to describe how you feel?*

*Does the card's message resonate with the question asked?
Why or why not? (Note that the answer can change when
you refer to this entry later.)*

What artwork, if any, on your selected card spoke to you?

✦ ·✦· journal entry ·✦· ✦

date _____ time _____

deck _____

_____
_____

card pulled _____

REFLECTION

_____
_____
_____
_____
_____
_____
_____
_____
_____
_____
_____

ADDITIONAL QUESTIONS FOR FURTHER REFLECTION

How do you interpret the message you received?

Can you use the oracle card's keyword in a sentence to describe how you feel?

Does the card's message resonate with the question asked? Why or why not? (Note that the answer can change when you refer to this entry later.)

What artwork, if any, on your selected card spoke to you?

◆ ·· journal entry ·· ◆

date _____   time _____

deck _____

QUESTION ASKED

_____

_____

card pulled _____

REFLECTION

_____

_____

_____

_____

_____

_____

_____

_____

_____

_____

ADDITIONAL QUESTIONS FOR FURTHER REFLECTION

How do you interpret the message you received?

*Can you use the oracle card's keyword in a sentence
to describe how you feel?*

*Does the card's message resonate with the question asked?
Why or why not? (Note that the answer can change when
you refer to this entry later.)*

What artwork, if any, on your selected card spoke to you?

✦ ·· journal entry ·· ✦

date _____ time _____

deck _____

QUESTION ASKED

_____
_____

card pulled _____

REFLECTION

_____
_____
_____
_____
_____
_____
_____
_____
_____
_____
_____

ADDITIONAL QUESTIONS FOR FURTHER REFLECTION

How do you interpret the message you received?

*Can you use the oracle card's keyword in a sentence
to describe how you feel?*

*Does the card's message resonate with the question asked?
Why or why not? (Note that the answer can change when
you refer to this entry later.)*

What artwork, if any, on your selected card spoke to you?

✦ ··journal entry·· ✦

date _____   time _____

deck _____

QUESTION ASKED

_____
_____

card pulled _____

REFLECTION

_____
_____
_____
_____
_____
_____
_____
_____
_____
_____
_____

ADDITIONAL QUESTIONS FOR FURTHER REFLECTION

How do you interpret the message you received?

*Can you use the oracle card's keyword in a sentence
to describe how you feel?*

*Does the card's message resonate with the question asked?
Why or why not? (Note that the answer can change when
you refer to this entry later.)*

What artwork, if any, on your selected card spoke to you?

✦ ∙∙ journal entry ∙∙ ✦

date _____ time _____

deck _____

QUESTION ASKED

_____

_____

card pulled _____

REFLECTION

_____

_____

_____

_____

_____

_____

_____

_____

_____

_____

_____

ADDITIONAL QUESTIONS FOR FURTHER REFLECTION

How do you interpret the message you received?

*Can you use the oracle card's keyword in a sentence
to describe how you feel?*

*Does the card's message resonate with the question asked?
Why or why not? (Note that the answer can change when
you refer to this entry later.)*

What artwork, if any, on your selected card spoke to you?

✦ ✦ journal entry ✦ ✦

date _____   time _____

deck _____

_____

_____

card pulled _____

REFLECTION

_____

_____

_____

_____

_____

_____

_____

_____

_____

_____

ADDITIONAL QUESTIONS FOR FURTHER REFLECTION

How do you interpret the message you received?

*Can you use the oracle card's keyword in a sentence
to describe how you feel?*

*Does the card's message resonate with the question asked?
Why or why not? (Note that the answer can change when
you refer to this entry later.)*

What artwork, if any, on your selected card spoke to you?

Index